The Alumni Board of Trustees of the University of Virginia Endowment Fund, Inc.,
generously supported the publication of this volume.

ISBN 978-0-8139-2854-8
Distributed by the University of Virginia Press
www.upress.virginia.edu

Printed by University of Virginia Printing and Copying Services

Meo Amico John Casteen

Contents

Like a Newton sublimely he soard
To a sumit before unattained,
New regions of science explord
And the palm of philosophy gaind,
With a spark that he caught from the skies
He displayd an unparalleld wonder,
And we saw with delight and surprise
That his rod could protect us from thunder
Oh had he been wise to pursue
The path which his talents designd,
What a tribute of praise had been due
To the teacher and freind of mankind,
But to covet political fame
Was in him a degrading ambition.
A spark which from Lucifer came
And kindld the blaze of sedition.
Let candour then write on his Urn
Here lies the renowned Inventor,
When the flames to the skies ought to burn
But inverted returns to the Center.

BENJAMIN FRANKLIN EPITAPH
inscription on an urn

National Archives of Scotland. NAS 02023 GD3331-7-3-00002.
New Register House. Edinburgh, Scotland

With the exception of the four lines referring to the lightning rod, Franklin could have equally written the preceding epitaph for Jefferson or Jefferson for himself. Both men believed that their true talent, genius, and gifts lie in the realms of science, but the exigencies of their country and their own sense of vanity had diverted the stream of destiny.

Preface

The century into which Thomas Jefferson was born was one of change and discovery. The way in which man viewed himself, his relationship with God, and his own position in "the system in which we are placed" evolved as radically and rapidly as in any period before. This era of systematic and scientific progress is generally referred to as the Enlightenment. Although variations on the Enlightenment manifested themselves in different ways in different countries, all versions shared the common belief in the supremacy of reason and the betterment of the human condition. The teachings of Francis Bacon and the illustrations of Isaac Newton made clear the import of reason and scientific method in man's attempts to understand the cosmos. The Scottish version of this new perspective stressed the concrete rather than the abstract, the utilitarian rather than the metaphysical, and solid scientific methodology rather than nebulous intellectual argumentation. It was in the tradition of the Scottish Enlightenment and the School of Common Sense Philosophy that Jefferson first encountered the expansion of science. The central tenet of this philosophy can be summed up in the word *improvement*. This process of enlightened improvement was all-encompassing, involving physical, moral, and aesthetic dimensions. The study of the divergent aspects of improvement was divided into natural and moral philosophy. Natural philosophy, often a synonym for science, dealt with the definition, description, and material causes of natural phenomena. Moral philosophy dealt with the metaphysics of values, meanings, and purposes —of what nature ultimately is and how we know it.[1]

In addition to improvement, the other major tenets of the Scottish Enlightenment were utility and scientific method. The consequence of this philosophy was a straightforward, optimistic outlook on the human condition. The true beginnings of this movement took their origins in the *Principia Mathematica* of Sir Isaac Newton. Newton's view of the logical and sequential structure of nature gave form and clarity not only to the physical aspects of the universe, but also to life itself. If there were a logical nature to being, if it were sequential, then it could be controlled. If the terror of the randomness of life were lessened, man could better direct the flow of his own destiny. The patterns of life had a natural, almost mathematical flow to them, and scientific method was the tool by which these patterns could be most effectively discerned. Once the pattern was discovered, a destructive flow could be altered into a beneficial stream, by reason and purpose. The result of acts that were purposefully useful was improvement. Although the first stage of improving life on earth pertained to man's physical well-being, the tenets of the Enlightenment extended this holistic approach to economic advancement, political stability, and mental and moral development.

The Enlightenment movements in Europe shared many common characteristics, but in Scotland they seem to have taken on a more democratic, more utilitarian, more scientific aspect. The movement and its benefits were not restricted to philosophes and ideologues but, like education in Scotland, were given much wider distribution. One of the first areas in which the leaders of the Scottish Enlightenment took an interest was the physical well-being of the people. The most evident way to make life better and the future more secure was to increase the food supply. The Scottish philosophers believed, as did Jefferson, that the key to a nation's self-sufficiency was the ability to feed its citizens. The first goal of improvement was agriculture. Scientific method, the first step of which is observation or data collection, was the means by which to discern the pattern that would lead to maximum production and distribution.

Statistical surveys in Scotland began in the late seventeenth century, when the enlightened elite, or virtuosi, commissioned clergymen to take statistical surveys of their parishes. In this way economic patterns could be discovered, natural resources could be used in a more effective way, productivity could be increased, and labor could be lessened. The result would benefit the whole society. Jefferson was an heir of this tradition. Throughout his life, Jefferson kept meticulous records, made repeated observations, and developed experiments and instituted projects compiling massive amounts of data. The basic concerns of all his investigations were utility and improvement.

Jefferson's most scientific famous work, *Notes on the State of Virginia*, was in many ways a reflection of the statistical surveys of Scotland. It was primarily a work of observations and data collections, marshaled in such a way as to make the information useful and applicable. Jefferson's objectives in *Notes on the State of Virginia* were not only to answer questions and make utile compilations, but also to support his political and social theories with scientific evidence. The Lewis and Clark Expedition likewise had political and social agenda, but it also resulted in one of the most expansive collections of raw scientific data compiled up to that time. This same exacting process is seen in the formation of the University of Virginia: the efficacious arrangement of subjects to be taught, educational methodology to be employed, professors to be hired, even the architectural positioning of buildings on the Grounds make philosophical statements.

The result of the importance of education in the Scottish psyche was the ironic situation that one of the best-educated societies in Europe dwelt in one of the most economically impoverished nations in the West. An unintended consequence of that plan was a proliferation of young educated Scots who came to America seeking opportunity and who stayed to tutor and teach their colonial cousins. These ubiquitous Scots spread the concept of equal opportunity and made the Common Sense philosophy of Thomas Reid the core tradition of the American Enlightenment[2] and what historian Perry Miller called "the official metaphysic of America."[3]

William Small, the remarkable young Scot who taught Thomas Jefferson and other early leaders of the Republic at the College of William and Mary, brought many tenets of Common Sense philosophy to Virginia. Two of the most important focused on science and democracy. If one were judged by his intellect, integrity, and industry, it opened up a society based on merit and established an aristocracy of intellect. While pragmatic subjects were of primary interest, Jefferson took the populist view concerning the subject of moral philosophy. He thought that "it lost time to attend lectures in this branch."[4] Jefferson expressed the essence of the Common Sense philosophy and his adherence to it in a letter to his grandson:

> *The moral sense, or conscience, is as much a part of a man as his leg or arm. It is given to all human beings in a stronger or weaker degree, as the force of members is given [them] in greater or less degree: it may be strengthened by exercise, as any particular limb of the body, this sense is submitted indeed in some degree to the guidance of reason, but it is small stock which is required for this: even a less one than we call Commonsense. State a moral case to a ploughman & a professor. The former will decide it as well & often better than the latter, because he has not been led astray by artificial rules.* [5]

Jefferson and others were often demonized for the atheistic tendencies attributed to those scientifically inclined. Scottish clergymen, however, were at the forefront of the Enlightenment movement in their country, and among the most vocal advocates of the Newtonian precepts. Instead of seeing science as a tool to diminish the relevance of God and the intercession of the church, they saw a cosmos ordered on scientific principles as an affirmation of the existence and power of God. The scientific method requires a null hypothesis to begin investigations. In this case the null hypothesis would be: "There is no God." The hypothesis would then be: "How can a universe so perfectly balanced and so logically constructed exist without the intervention and inspiration of an all-powerful God?" That God allows man the opportunity to better his life and the lives of his fellow creatures through science is not a refutation of his being but rather an affirmation.

Throughout his life, Jefferson promoted science, utility, and improvement, the hallmarks of the Common Sense philosophy. In everything he did, he sought something that led to the betterment of the lives of his fellow citizens, accomplished by reasoned and useful means, following scientific principles.

In 1758, the Scottish thinker John Gregory and his cousin, Thomas Reid, founded the Aberdeen Philosophical Society, which stressed the scientific concerns of improvement—the present and pragmatic, not the implications for moral philosophy, namely the hereafter and the abstract. Out of the discussions of this intellectual club rose the practical foundations for the School of Common Sense. These precepts were passed on to Thomas Jefferson through John Gregory's protégé, William Small, Jefferson's only professor at William and Mary. This foundation, in part, created in Jefferson and in many of his classmates a lifelong devotion to scientific method, utility, and the improvement in the station of their fellow man.

The Wren Building at the College of William and Mary.
Reproduced by permission from the Virginia Historical Society, Richmond, Virginia.

This book will take a look at various branches of science in which Jefferson was immersed and to which he made lasting contributions. It will also examine how science shaped his views on the politics, religion, economics, and social developments in his own country. Although this work is not all-inclusive, it will examine broad aspects of Jefferson's scientific interests and his utilitarian applications. The first of all the sciences for Jefferson was agriculture, to which he was attached "by inclination as well as by conviction that it is the most useful of occupations of man."[6] Jefferson was more a promoter than an innovator in this field, introducing new and useful plants and livestock into America, advocating the study and practice of agriculture as a science, and bringing forth his original invention of the mathematically precise "Mouldboard Plough of Least Resistance."

In 1761, famed natural historian George Louis Leclerc, Comte de Buffon, posited the theory of New World degeneracy. According to Buffon's *Histoire Naturelle*, species of flora and fauna were both less numerous and of smaller size in the New World than in the Old World, that the inhabitants of the New World were of less valor and antiquity than those of the Old World, and that any living species transported to the New World from the Old World would, in time, degenerate both in size and strength. Inflamed by the audacious insult to his own country, the scientific inaccuracy of Buffon's methods, and the potential injury to immigration to America, Jefferson responded by pioneering a number of novel branches of science.

Jefferson investigated Native American history, culture, origin, and language as a means of scientifically repudiating the assertions of Buffon and his followers. In the study of the history of indigenous Americans, he conducted an archaeological dig for the purpose of obtaining knowledge rather than treasures. In the process, he developed the scientific methodology of stratification, which is the foundation of modern archeological techniques. Because of this innovation, he is often called the "Father of American Archaeology."

To counter Buffon's imputations against Native Americans, including immoral and cowardly behavior, lazy habits and weak intellects, and racial immaturity, Jefferson helped to develop the nascent disciplines of anthropology, ethnology, and comparative linguistics. Constantin François de Chassebœuf, the Comte de Volney, a pioneer in scientific anthropology and a friend of Jefferson, studied the cultures and religions of Native Americans to demonstrate their origins and antiquity. In the process, scientific anthropologic techniques were established. Also Jefferson spent thirty years collecting Indian vocabularies to establish a scientifically objective foundation for the correlation of the relationship between the natives of America and peoples of Asia.

Humans, however, were not the only avenue of uncovering the antiquity of the New World. Although fossils had been reported by Spanish conquistadors in North America as early as 1519, it was not until the degeneracy controversy generated by Buffon that intense interest in them arose among the educated elite and that a more scientific approach in paleontological studies was required. When Jefferson was inaugurated as the president of the American Philosophical Society, he presented his report "Memoir on the Megalonyx" to the assembled group and published his findings in the *Transactions of the American Philosophical Society* in an article entitled "A Memoir on the Discovery of certain Bones of a Quadruped of the Clawed Kind in the Western Parts of Virginia." Throughout his life, he would continue to support and promote investigations into this area of research by encouraging the artist and natural historian Charles Willson Peale in his excavation of a mammoth and instructing Lewis and Clark to seek out fossils during their expedition west. His contributions to this branch of science have caused some to name Jefferson the "Father of American Paleontology."

Another facet of science that engaged Jefferson's early attention was the health-promoting virtues of scientific medicine. When only twenty-three, Jefferson was inoculated for smallpox. Investigations into the epidemics of smallpox and yellow fever convinced him of the salutary value of fresh air and cleansing sunshine. He purposefully incorporated these concepts into his architectural plans, designing rooms with windows that admitted carefully calculated amounts of sunshine and air flow and advocating small and separate buildings surrounded by fresh air rather than massive structures with cramped and unhealthy conditions. Jefferson's design for the University of Virginia followed these tenets, which may have had their origins in the innovative prisons and hospitals of England and France.

In his capacity as minister to France, secretary of state, and president of the United States, Jefferson knew well the importance of ensuring the security of diplomatic dispatches and maintaining secrecy in regard to sensitive matters. Jefferson's endeavors as a scientific spymaster include his many and elaborate systems for coding messages, his recruitment of men of science and frontier scouts as secret observers for the state, and his remarkable cipher wheel for passing along secret documents and missives.

The final chapter of this book will offer a broader summary of

Jefferson's scientific interests and accomplishments, supported by such evidence as the numerous scientific encomiums and honors he accumulated, the profound nature and astonishing variety of his scientific publications, the contents of his library, and the scientific equipment he acquired. This book also offers a fresh view of Monticello, the University of Virginia, and even Jefferson's own gravestone as testimonials to his devotion to science.

Editorial Method

The guiding principle behind the textual editing of this work has been to follow Julian Boyd's advice as reflected in the title of his article on this subject, "God's Altar Needs Not Our Pollishings" *New York History*. Vol. XXXIX (January 1958). All citations have been left as originally written in primary source documents or as recorded where the originals have not been available, unless editorial intervention was unavoidable. With this in mind, please note the following peculiarities of Jefferson's style.

Spelling and misspelling have been retained as written. Archaic and obsolete forms have not been altered, frequently past tenses reflect a -'d instead of an –ed, and Jefferson systematically rendered its as it's.

Punctuation also was sometimes erratic. Jefferson, perhaps adopting the editorial style of his legal mentor George Wythe, did not capitalize the first word in a sentence unless the word was a proper noun or first person singular pronoun. After numbers Jefferson frequently inserted a period; virgules and periods often elide. Not expressed in citations was the macron that Jefferson often employed over mid-sentences, proper names, and titles (particularly mr).

Words inserted into the original document by the author are noted by carets < >; words omitted by the author but essential for understanding the text are expressed with brackets [ ]; torn or missing text and illegible or unintelligible words are notated.

1

Agriculture

It is from the tillers of the soil that springs the best citizens,
the staunchest soldiers; and theirs are the enduring rewards
which are most grateful and least envied. Such as devote
themselves to that pursuit are least given to evil counsels.
—Marcus Porcius Cato the Censor

The earliest surviving letter that is known to be by Thomas Jefferson
was written in 1760, when he was sixteen. He was already employing the
tools of science and utility to make his case to attend college in distant
Williamsburg. "[A]s long as I stay in the Mountains the Loss of one
fourth of my Time is inevitable," he wrote, "and likewise my Absence
will be in great Measure put a Stop to so much Company, and by that
Means lessen the Expences of the Estate in House-Keeping."[1] His interest in science and mathematics, likely engendered by his surveying father, increased with exposure to the correct teachings of James Maury
and was cultivated at William and Mary by his erudite professor, William
Small, and the enlightened companions of the *partie quarrae.*

When Thomas Jefferson wrote to Pierre Samuel du Pont de
Nemours, "Nature intended me for the tranquill pursuits of science, by
rendering them my supreme delight,"[2] he was expressing a characteristic

that was innate, not instilled. In 1773, when his best friend and brother-in-law, Dabney Carr, died, Jefferson recorded even this sad event in mathematical and utilitarian terms.

> May.22: 2 hands grubbed the Grave yard 80.f.sq =
> 1/7 of an acre in 3 ? hours so that one would have
> done it in 7. Hours, and would grub an acre in
> 49.hours = 4. Days.[3]

Among the subjects that most closely engaged Jefferson's "canine" appetite for knowledge were agriculture, archeology, astronomy, botany, zoology, paleontology, comparative linguistics, mathematics, physics, chemistry, mineralogy, meteorology, metrology, mechanics, optics, entomology, natural history, geology, and geography. But of these "tranquill pursuits," none stands out more than agriculture.

Jefferson described agriculture as "a science of the first order. It counts among its handmaidens the most respectable sciences, such as Chemistry, Natural Philosophy, Mechanics, Mathematics generally, Natural History, Botany."[4] In 1826, he informed John Patton Emmet, one of the first professors at the University of Virginia, that the "allotments to your school are Botany, Zoology, Mineralogy, Chemistry, Geology, and Rural Economy. The last, however, need not be considered a distinct branch, but as one that might be treated in seasonable alliance with the kindred subjects of Chemistry, Botany and Zoology."[5]

Jefferson's interest in the science of agriculture was closely tied to the ideal of an agrarian nation. In a letter to John Jay, Jefferson wrote, "Cultivators of the earth are the most valuable citizens. They are the most vigorous, the most independent, the most virtuous, and they are tied to their country, and wedded to its liberty and interests, by the most lasting bonds." From a political as well as moral standpoint, he considered the yeomen a much more reliable foundation of citizenry than those engaged in manufacturing goods: "Comparing the characters of the two classes, I find the former the most valuable citizens. I consider the class of artificers as the panders of vice, and the instruments by which the liberties of the country are overturned."[6]

Agriculture as a science also endeared itself to Jefferson on a personal level. While serving as minister to France, Jefferson wrote to Lafayette, "I am never satiated with rambling through the fields and farms, examining culture and cultivators, with a degree of curiosity which makes some take me to be a fool, and others to be much wiser than I am."[7] Six years later, and seven years before he would become the president of the United States, he wrote both that the "motion of my blood no longer keeps time with the tumult of the world" and that he longed only for the love of his family, the society of his neighbors and books, and "the wholesome occupations of my farm."[8]

But even a matter so close to his heart, Jefferson approached with scientific method. Agriculture was an area that stimulated and employed a diversity of Jefferson's greatest scientific interests and abilities and the first object for "improvement" in the Scottish Enlightenment model. Improving production on the farm might involve the fields of mathematics, botany, zoology, chemistry, mineralogy, meteorology, astronomy, and geology. Monticello became an agricultural laboratory; the aim of experimentation was to increase production and decrease labor, to make greater the profits and lessen the waste, to have all plans and implementations both complete and complement one another.

Jefferson sought to improve agricultural output by introducing new crops and livestock to American farms; by advancing agricultural techniques such as soil conservation, crop rotation, contour plowing, and livestock management; by advocating for inventions and innovations that would increase productivity and self-sufficiency; by protecting crops and livestock from destructive pests; and by the creation of agricultural societies that would share discoveries and promote the latest methods. He even toyed with the advanced theories of Dr. Jan Ingenhousz, who at one time advocated that "vegetation might be promoted by occasioning streams of electrical fluid to pass through a plant."[9] It is said that Jefferson cultivated 170 varieties of fruits and 330 different kinds of vegetables (including forty types of beans, two dozen kinds of English peas, and seventeen types of lettuce). He also studied the impact of light on the color of living things.

While journeying through southern France and northern Italy, Jefferson was always on the alert for ways to better the rural economy of his country "because the resemblance of their climate to the southern parts of the United States, authorizes us to presume we may adopt any of their article of culture which we would wish for."[10]

Viniculture seems to have preoccupied much of his attention, for he carefully examined the soil and observed the climate throughout his tour of southern France and northern Italy. Although he was later to try his hand in this industry, he wrote, "The culture of the vine is not desirable in lands capable of producing any thing else. It is a species of desperate gambling too, wherein, whether you make much or little, you are equally ruined. The middling crop alone is the saving point, and that the seasons seldom hit. Accordingly we see much wretchedness amidst this class of cultivators."[11]

He found that Italian rice, although it was "shorter, thicker, and less white…[nevertheless] it preserved it's form better,"[12] was preferred in Paris to Carolina rice and sold for a higher price. He assumed at first that the variation in the quality of the rice was caused by a machine called a rice beater, which husked the grains. After Jefferson had carefully observed the Italian husking device in operation, however, he concluded, "the machine to be absolutely the same with that used in Carolina."[13] Jefferson came to the opinion that "the rice of Lombardy…is of a different species from that of Carolina, different in form, in colour, and in quality."[14] Because the rice from Vercelli was considered the best in Italy and commanded the highest prices, the exportation of the seed was strictly prohibited. Jefferson decided to smuggle the agricultural contraband out of the country.

> I could only bring off as much as my coat and surtout
> pockets could hold. I took measures with a muletier to
> run a couple of sacks across the Appenines to Genoa,
> but have not great dependence on it's success.[15]

In order that the furtive cargo would not be lost in transit or confiscated by a zealous government, Jefferson devised a meticulous and surefire plan for the arrival of the unhusked grain in South Carolina. He wrote to William Drayton, "A part of this I have addressed to you by way of London; a part comes with this letter; and I shall send another parcel by some other conveyance to prevent the danger of miscarriage. Any one of them arriving safe may serve to put in seed."[16]

The other agricultural imports that he encouraged were the caper and the olive tree. He found the caper very useful in sauces. Although "the tenderest plant," it could be easily protected and "is the most certain of it's fruit."[17] But it was for the olive tree that Jefferson had the greatest admiration: "Of all the gifts of heaven to man, it is next to the most precious, if it not be the most precious."[18] He observed that olive trees produce good crops within twenty years, could be grown in any dry soil, would live for as long as two hundred years, and that other crops could be cultivated between the trees. In addition, "they afford an easy but constant employment thro' the year…having been myself an eyewitness to the blessing which this tree sheds on the poor, I never had my wishes so kindled for the introduction of any article of new culture into our own country."[19]

Due to Jefferson's promotion, several hundred olive trees were sent to Charleston in 1793, and in 1813, he had five hundred saplings sent to South Carolina from Aix.[20] Despite Jefferson's encouragement and the South Carolina Agricultural Society's willingness to experiment, the attempt to establish the olive industry was unsuccessful. The delicate caper met a similar fate. Jefferson also promoted breadfruit, and he had been "long endeavoring to procure the Cork tree from Europe, but without success."[21] He continued unabated to search for new varieties of both fruits and vegetables from not only Europe and the East but also the unexplored regions of the western parts of the continent. Jefferson was happy to swap with others and, in 1801, sent squash and pumpkin seeds with planting instructions to Philip Mazzei and requested in return "any plants of good fruit, and especially of peaches and *eating grapes*."[22] In 1804, Meriwether Lewis sent cuttings of Osage plums and apples back to the Jefferson White House with a description of the fruit and the particulars of their usefulness.[23]

Although Jefferson's attempts at introducing new crops were not always successful, nevertheless his efforts fostered experimentation and exchange. Networks of interested farmers grew into societies of mutual benefit. He also promoted the importation of new varieties of livestock. Two of his most aggressive projects involved Merino sheep and sheep dogs.

The continuing hostile relationship with England and the imperative to be self-sustaining compelled the young country to improve the quality of manufactured goods. In Jefferson's view, upgrading the cotton and wool industries would be vital to this endeavor, and Merino sheep, which had a reputation for both fine wool and delicious meat, looked especially promising. The sheep were raised in the mountains bordering Spain and Portugal and commanded high prices. Their exportation was strictly prohibited. Neveretheless, several enterprising Americans—Robert Livingston of New York, David Humphreys of Connecticut, and the du Ponts of Delaware—were able to obtain a few of the prized sheep. Jefferson himself ordered a Merino ram through the du Ponts, but it died in transit to the United States.

Jefferson wrote to the American consul in Madrid, "An American vessel...proposes to touch at some port of Spain with the view of obtaining Merino sheep to be brought to our country. the necessity we are under, & the determination we have formed of emancipating ourselves from a dependence on foreign countries for manufactures which may be advantageously established among ourselves, has produced a very general desire to improve the quality of our wool by the introduction of the Merino race of sheep."[24]

Knowing that "Congress could not, by our Constitution give one dollar for all in Spain, because that kind of power has not been given them,"[25] Jefferson suggested that this be accomplished by private means. Joseph Dougherty, who was in the process of obtaining the sheep, enclosed a sample of wool,[26] which Jefferson found fine. A receipt of May 1810 shows that it cost Dougherty $39.35 to transport four Merino sheep from Lisbon to Alexandria; the actual price of the sheep is not mentioned.[27] Appalled to learn that four Merino sheep had been sold for the extraordinary price of $6,000, Jefferson wrote to James Madison that he had "been so disgusted with the scandalous extortions lately practised in the sale of these animals" that he wished to "put to shame" the gouging importers and "to excite by better example" a way to help their countrymen.[28] He requested that Madison formulate a plan and that to commence the matter he would "throw out the first idea, to be modified, or postponed, or whatever" Madison thought appropriate:

Give all the full blooded males we can raise to the different counties of our state, one to each, as fast as we can furnish them. and as there must be some rules of priority, for the distribution, let us begin with our own counties, which are contiguous & nearly central to the state, & proceed, circle after circle, till we have given a ram to every county. this will take about 7. years. …we may ask some known character in each county to have a small society formed which shall receive the animal & prescribe rules for his care and government.[29]

In a postscript to Pierre Samuel du Pont de Nemours, Jefferson requested, "If you return to us bring a couple of pair of true-bred shepherd dogs. You will add a valuable possession to a country now beginning to pay great attention to raising sheep."[30] This breed was known for being "perfectly trained to the business" of keeping the sheep contained. As a result, French farmers "have now the benefit of as fine as pastures as can be, the dog keeping them from the grain in the same inclosures."[31] Having obtained and raised some of these dogs, he wrote to his neighbor, "besides their wonderful sagacity & neverceasing attention to what they are taught to do, they appear to have more courage than I had before supposed that race to possess. they make the best farm dogs or house dogs I have ever seen."[32] The Marquis de Lafayette sent a pair of sheep dogs to Jefferson, adding that they "have been carefully multiplied, and are spreading in this and the neighboring states where the increase of our sheep is greatly attended to."[33]

Don Pedro, Merino ram. *Courtesy of Hagley Museum and Library.*

As with his other schemes for money making, this one also was doomed. Within a decade of the end of the War of 1812, the importation of the Merino sheep had become so accelerated that the value of the stock dramatically reduced. In addition, Americans found the wool too fine and expensive for everyday wear, and the sheep were disappointingly small in size. By the end of the decade, the Merino began to make their appearance in butcher shops.

Other aspects of Jefferson's scientific approach to rural economy included the systematic manipulation of the soil and the introduction of new inventions to increase the productivity of the farm. In the first category, the three most significant innovations were horizontal or contour plowing, crop rotation, and the use of gypsum in the process of fertilization. Jefferson found that the traditional rotation of tobacco and corn depleted the soil of its nutrients and contributed significantly to erosion. Echoing Locke, Jefferson wrote to Charles Willson Peale, "the spontaneous energies of the earth are a gift of nature, but they require the labor of man to direct their operation."[34] Praising the technique developed by his son-in-law, Thomas Mann Randolph, he wrote:

> we have had the most devastating rain which has ever fallen within my knolege. three inches of water fell in the space of about an hour. every hollow of every hill presented a torrent which swept everything before it. I have never seen the fields so much injured. mr. Randolph's farm is the only one which has not suffered; his horizontal furrows arrested the water at every step, till it was absorbed, or at least had deposited the soil it had taken up. everybody in the neighborhood is adopting his method of ploughing, except the tenants who have no interest in the preservation of the soil.[35]

To Jefferson, the great advantages of this system were that the plowing would follow the natural contours of the hills. In rainstorms, instead of the soil running straight down into the rivers, it would be caught in the next furrow and would create a small reservoir, which would continue to nurture the growing plants while preventing erosion of the fields.

Tobacco, the major cash crop, so significantly exhausted the soil that it was often more expedient to open up new fields rather than to try to rehabilitate the old ones. Although land was plentiful, it was not infinite. The alternative to moving constantly was to rejuvenate the soil, and Jefferson thought this best accomplished by crop rotation and chemical fertilizers. Crop rotation was not a new concept, but the concept of alternative crops to enrich the soil instead of the fallow process was. In 1794, he wrote to John Taylor:

> and though I observe your strictures on the rotation of crops, yet it appears in this I differ from you only in words. You keep half your lands in culture, the other half at nurse; so I propose to do. Your scheme indeed requires only four years and mine six. … My years of rest however are employed, two of them in producing clover, yours in volunteer herbage. … Indeed I think that the important improvement … is the substitution of clover crops instead of unproductive fallows: and the demonstration that lands are more enriched by clover than by volunteer herbage or fallows: and clover crops are highly valuable.[36]

The rotation included wheat followed by turnips in the first year. The turnips could be used for fodder for the sheep. In the second year, corn and potatoes were followed by vetch, again used for enrichment and fodder. Peas or potatoes were planted in the third year; rye and clover in the fourth year; clover alone in the fifth; and clover in the spring of the sixth year followed by vetch. In the spring of the seventh year, the vetch was turned and the wheat restarted. Though it was efficacious, even Jefferson admitted that this deliberate process was "slow in it's operation." It failed to catch on in an era of abundant land, cheap labor, and the desire for cash crops. [37]

Jefferson also turned his attention to the preservation of crops against the "bite and tred" of livestock and insects. He was greatly impressed with the efficacy of sheep dogs in restricting the trespassing of sheep and also brought into practice the use of natural fences and the ha-ha ditch. At

Monticello, he substituted "rows of Peach trees" in place of cross fences, which relieved him of the "labor and expence…very sensibly felt on account of the scarcity and distance of timber."[38] The ha-ha fence also required little maintenance; it consisted of a ditch–much in the manner of a Roman military fossa–with wooded slats lying overtop. This prevented livestock from crossing over into areas producing crops, while leaving the garden vistas uninterrupted by artificial barriers.[39]

Another threat to crops that concerned Jefferson was the Hessian fly, which first appeared near Flatbush, New York, near where the Hessian troops landed. From there, the infestation spread about twenty miles a year, he noted, "more or less according to the winds."[40] Jefferson wrote to his son-in-law that a "Committee of the Philosophic society is charged with collecting materials for the natural history of the Hessian fly."[41] He immediately began detailing the biological minutiae of the insect and the progress of its destruction[42] and reported his findings to the American Philosophical Society on June 7, 1792:[43]

Ha-ha fence.
Illustration by John James, 1712.

> The Hessian fly remains on the ground among the stubble of the old wheat. At ploughing time for sowing the new crop they rise in swarms before the plough horses. Soon after the wheat comes up they lay an egg in it, of the size of a nit, and will crack like it. … In the spring they begin to grow. [I saw them just below the highlands on the 21st. of May in the worm state, about as long as a grain of rye, and one third it's volume. White, smooth and transparent.] In June the Chrysalis bursts and the insect comes out, brown like a flax seed, a little longer, and with wings. The egg is found from

the joint nearest the ground. …The stem decays in that part, turns yellow, the blades become erect, and the plant dies.[44]

Jefferson also relates that the Hessian fly attacks fruit as well as grain: "Bartram here tells me that it is one & the same insect which by depositing it's egg in the young plumbs, apricots, nectarines & peaches renders them gummy & good for nothing."[45] Jefferson in his report took a scientific approach to the problem. He identified all the dimensions of the insect anatomically, he precisely described its life cycle and destructive stages, and reported the ways in which its destruction can be limited or eliminated.

In the area of agricultural inventions, Jefferson applied his genius to the improvement of technology rather than its inception. In 1793, he turned his attention to the adaptation of a recent Scottish threshing machine because of its utility; he wrote, "South of the Patowmac, the finest wheat country in America."[46] If the wheat was not threshed out within three or four weeks after cutting, "it is destroyed all of a sudden by the weevil," but if it is threshed immediately and "kept in its chaff, it is secure against insect," Jefferson observed.[47] For the farmer it was a difficult choice in

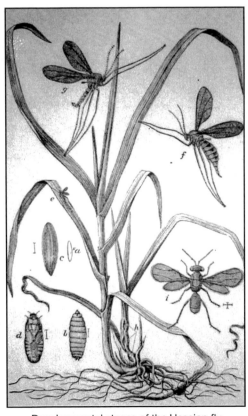

Developmental stages of the Hessian fly.
E. L. Trouvelot. Prepared for A. S. Packard, "Hessian Fly: Its Ravages, Habits, and Means of Preventing its Increase," United States Entomological Commission, Bulletin #4 (1880).

that the process of threshing by hand or treading by horse was so time consuming that it "loses the season" for planting the next year's crop. "Very frequently we are in the dilemma of sacrificing either the crop of the present, or that of the next year."[48]

In the spring of 1793, Jefferson wrote to James Madison that he had received a model of the Scottish threshing machine from Mr. Thomas Pinckney, who "had been to see one work, which with 2. horses got out 8. bushels of wheat an hour."[49] By comparison, Jefferson was assured the model he designed "gets out 8 quarters [64 bushels] of oats an hour with 4. horses."[50] He informed James Adair that in the South the threshing machine was "as valuable as the discovery of the grain itself" and encouraged him to send the Scottish workman to Virginia, where "he may quickly make a fortune by building machines."[51] Jefferson also adapted a hemp break, writing to Charles Willson Peale that the device "breaks & beats about 80. lb a day with a single horse."[52]

Although Jefferson was most adept at refining inventions already in existence, his mouldboard plow of least resistance is considered an original innovation. On April 19, 1788, while making a tour through Holland and France, Jefferson noted that the awkward mouldboard plow used by peasants "leads one to consider what should be it's form. The offices of the mould board are to receive the sod after the share has cut under it, to raise it gradually and reverse it."[53]

To remedy this defect, Jefferson worked out mathematical equations and drew geometric representations on the backs of bills and scraps of

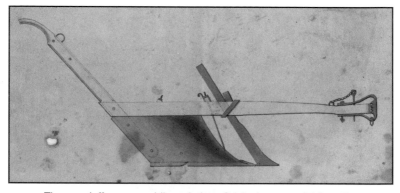

Thomas Jefferson mouldboard plow. Original manuscript from the Coolidge Collection of Thomas Jefferson Manuscripts.
Courtesy of the Massachusetts Historical Society.

paper. Lured by other scientific enticements, and encouraged by his nation to undertake unwanted political obligations, Jefferson put aside his enthusiasm for the mouldboard for some time. The first model was made for his son-in-law Thomas Mann Randolph in the winter of 1790.[54]

On November 30, 1793, on the cusp of what he believed was his retirement from government duty, Jefferson bought a Pennsylvania barnshare plow from George Logan as an experimental frame for his first full-scale mouldboard. Jefferson's design used mathematical principles to decrease the resistance the plow encountered as it raised the clods of earth and inverted them. In addition to reducing the effort required for man and beast, this would allow more land to be worked in a shorter time, and it would provide a deeper furrow. A deeper furrow made possible an earlier planting and harvest, which in turn might ameliorate the problem of the weevil or permit multiple harvests.

The main requirements for the invention were its "simplicity & cheapness of construction, ease of repair, & the perfect performance of it's offices."[55] Jefferson claimed that his mouldboard could be reproduced by the "most bungling carpenter"[56] and that there would not be one "hair's breadth difference between one easily reproduced mouldboard and the next."[57] He explained in a letter to Jonathan Williams that he designed the plow according to mathematical principles, that he had conferred with David Rittenhouse with respect to its construction, and only wished "for one of those instruments used in England for measuring the force exerted in the draught of different ploughs &c. that I might compare the resistance of my mould board with others."[58]

In 1798, he wrote to Sir John Sinclair, president of the London Board of Agriculture, that he was quite satisfied with his design: "an experience of 5. years has enabled me to say it answers in practice to what it promises in theory."[59] The letter to Sinclair is amazing not only for its detailed description of the mouldboard plow, but also for the remarkable breadth of Jefferson's knowledge of the application of science to agriculture. In this one letter he tells Sinclair about the use of new chemistry in the application of manure, the advantages of the potato, experiments with different strains of wheat, a new seeding machine that made the vital production of clover more expedient, and the development of contour plowing.

If Jefferson approved of his mouldboard design, he was not alone. In 1798, Benjamin Latrobe wrote Jefferson that he was "astonished at the performance"[60] of the plow. Lord Sheffield praised the device as "a beautiful simplicity in the means of uniformly producing the same product"[61] and was informed by the American Charge d'Affairs in Paris that the Abbé Hauy had pronounced the plow to be "mathematically exact, and incapable of further improvement."[62] In April 1805, the Société d'Agriculture de la Seine awarded Jefferson a gold medal for his invention.

Over the years, Jefferson had more than twenty models of his mouldboard produced and sent to friends, family, colleagues, and institutions. William Strickland, a frequent correspondent, visiting from England in 1795, even received one Jefferson had made himself.[63] Members of the New York State Agricultural Society declared his practical method of exact duplication one of the most valuable contributions any one man had made toward the perfecting of plows.[64] A description of the mouldboard was widely disseminated after this publication, both at home and abroad, and Jefferson continued to encourage its use.[65]

Yet, in spite of the long years of experimenting and testing, of corresponding and promoting, of praises and prizes from various institutions and individuals, Jefferson's plow was never embraced by farmers. In 1868, the New York Agricultural Society declared that it had never seen or heard of "a single plow having been made on the principle laid down by Mr. Jefferson in his day, except those made by himself."[66]

2

Archaeology, Anthropology, Ethnology, and Comparative Linguistics

*The moment a person forms a theory, his imagination sees
in every object only the tracts which favor that theory.*
—THOMAS JEFFERSON TO CHARLES THOMSON,
SEPTEMBER 20, 1787

Jefferson's interest in Native American history, culture, and languages
led to the initiation and advancement of several fields of scientific study,
among them archaeology, ethnology, anthropology, and comparative linguistics. One of the main catalysts for Jefferson's exploration of these
areas was his desire to counter the degenerative theories of the celebrated
French natural historian, the Comte de Buffon, who was convinced that
the physical environment of the New World had the effect of stunting
both animal and vegetative growth. According to the eminent natural
historian, the American continent had only recently emerged from the
sea and, being covered with swamps and morasses and jungles, emitted
noxious airs. As a result, American plants were weaker and less utile than
those in the Old World; animals were smaller and less aggressive than
their European counterparts; Native Americans were physically, men-

tally, and morally inferior; and even those animals and persons transferred to America would undergo progressive degeneration. Based on the dicta of some of the most renowned authorities on natural history, these ideas soon gained wide acceptance.[1]

Buffon's theory first appeared in *Histoire Naturelle* in 1761 and was taken up and expanded upon by other European philosophes. The Dutch philosopher Cornelius de Pauw contended that animals indigenous to America were a thousand times less dangerous than those native to Asia and Africa, that animals imported to America became incrementally weaker and more debilitated, and, more alarmingly, that this phenomenon also affected settlers migrating to the continent. The Abbé

Comte de Buffon.
Oil painting by François-Hubert Drouais (1725-1775).

Raynal asserted that Native Americans were endowed with less strength and courage and were less lively and affectionate than the people of the old continent, and because of the indolence of men, women were saddled with excessive toil. With direct reference to Buffon, he argued that the people of America suffered from an organic imperfection that rendered them perpetually childlike.[2] The degeneracy theory became *au courant* among writers and academics of the time, and the potential damage of this "irresponsible slander" became immediately apparent to Thomas Jefferson, John Adams, Benjamin Franklin, and other Americans.

In 1780, the Secretary of the French Legation, François Marbois, requested statistical accounts of each American state. For Virginia, this task happily fell to Jefferson, who "had always made it a practice whenever an opportunity occurred of obtaining any information of our country, which might be of use to me in any station public or private, to commit it to writing."[3] It seemed to him the perfect time to take the scattered notes, collected on "loose papers, bundled up without order" and "to embody their substance." It also presented an ideal opportunity to refute Buffon. Jefferson's *Notes on the State of Virginia* would use precise statistical evidence to disprove Buffon's claims, which were based on undocumented data and specious theories. Buffon's ideas not only painted an insulting picture of the promise that was America, but also threatened to undercut economic and political growth in the new republic. The insinuation that America was a geographic location that, by its very nature, caused all forms of life to become weak and inferior would surely discourage both investment and immigration.[4]

Jefferson addressed the charge of degeneracy and inferiority of Native Americans in an almost clinical manner. Buffon's contention that the American Indian was inferior to the European or Asian could be countered in two ways. The first was to establish the origin of the native races, and the second was to describe accurately their physical, mental, and moral character, as well as the nature of their society. The first path led Jefferson to groundbreaking developments in archaeology and comparative linguistics; the second to innovations in the fields of anthropology and ethnology. If it could be established that the aborigines of North America were not a separate race but rather connected to Asian and European stock, then Buffon's theory of an inherently inferior race would be undermined. If it were established that differences in customs and mores were due to societal factors and not the debilitating effects of the physical environment, the notion of continental degeneracy would be discredited.

Ancient Origins of Native Americans

Even before Buffon's statements concerning the indigenous peoples of America circulated, there was a great deal of speculation regarding their heritage. One theory, reportedly first articulated by Amerigo Vespucci, named the lost tribes of Israel as the progenitors of the Native Americans. Several eighteenth-century authors defended the proposition, including an Indian trader named James Adair who pointed to the belief in one God, the division of society into tribes, the theocratic nature of government, and similarities in language as a proof of the connection between the two peoples.[5] Jefferson was aware of the "Mexican tradition," which made either the Aztecs or the Toltecs the ancestors of the North American tribes. Benjamin Smith Barton, nephew of David Rittenhouse, opined that the Indians had derived from the Toltecs, who, in turn, were progeny of the Danes.[6] Dr. Andrew Turnbull maintained that the Creek Indians descended from Carthaginians whose ships strayed from Hannibal's fleet.[7] Strangely, Jefferson expressed to Edward Rutledge in 1788 that he found "nothing impossible in this conjecture."[8] Another theory linked the Indians to an Alexandrian fleet lost in the fourth century B.C.[9] One tradition claimed that America was settled, at least in part, in 1170 by Prince Madoc of Wales. It was said, according to historian Anthony F. C. Wallace, "that he sailed westward in ten ships and never returned...and that the adventurers reached America and left descendants among the Indians."[10] Isaac Stewart, one of the many captives of the Indian Wars, claimed that he came across a tribe seven hundred miles up the Red River speaking Welsh and with documents written in ink. Unfortunately all the members of the party were either illiterate or ignorant of the Welsh language.[11] Other candidates included Canaanites, Phoenicians, the followers of a mythic prince of Atlantis, Egyptians, and a group of Tyrian sailors from the time of King Solomon.

Jefferson himself seems to have favored the theory of a crossing from Asia: "I suppose the settlement of our continent is of the most remote antiquity. The similitude between it's inhabitants and those of the Eastern parts of Asia renders it probable that ours are descended, or they from ours."[12] Jefferson's views may well have been influenced by an American traveling through Russia, who reported to Jefferson "how universaly and circumstantialy the Tartars resemble the aborigines of America. ... They are the same people—the most ancient, the most numerous of any other, and had not a small sea divided them, they would still be known by the *same name*. The cloak of civilization sits as ill upon them as our American tartars."[13]

In spite of all the speculation, Jefferson, wanting to have all the data necessary to make an informed decision concerning this matter, simply proclaimed, "ignoro"—I don't know. His search for evidence led him to the excavation of a small burial mound near his home on the Rivanna River in 1780.

Father of American Archaeology

The word archaeology was likely coined by the physician Jacob Spon, who traveled extensively throughout Asia Minor and Greece; Johann Joachim Winckelmann (1717-1768) has been called the "Father of Archaeology." Both men concentrated their studies on the art of the ancient world. Winckelmann's book, *Geschichte der Kunst des Altertums*, was based on the reports of diggers at Herculaneum and Pompeii, who were primarily in search of art treasures for royal collections.[14] As C. W. Ceram has noted, early archaeology was "in no sense a study of the whole *culture* —whereas modern archaeologists regard it as their supreme task."[15] Jefferson's excavation of the Indian burial ground near his home in Charlottesville may well have been the first scientific examination of remains with a cultural rather than artistic focus and earned him the title of "Father of American Archaeology."[16]

Renowned archaeologist Sir Mortimer Wheeler[17] looked back with amazement at the scientific techniques Jefferson used:

He describes the situation of the mound in relation to natural features and evidences of human occupation. He detects components of geological interest in its materials and traces their sources. He indicates the stratigraphical features of the skeletal remains. And he relates his evidence objectively to current theories. No mean achievement for a busy statesman in 1784![18]

All of these elements represented a new approach based on scientific method and careful analysis for the purpose of obtaining objective information about culture rather than artifacts and curiosities for collections. It also established a number of scientific traditions in the field of archaeology, such as examination of relevant topographic, geologic, and environmental factors surrounding the locale of the investigation; the use of stratigraphy to establish chronology; and shifting the focus of archaeology to obtain objective physical evidence on which to base sound and solid conclusions about ancient cultures.

Jefferson's detailed account of the dig begins with a precise picture of the site and its surroundings:

It was situated on the low grounds of the Rivanna,

about two miles above its principal fork, and opposite to some hills, on which had been an Indian town. It was of a spheroidical form, of about 40 feet diameter at the base, and had been of about twelve feet altitude, though now reduced by the plough to seven and a half, having been under cultivation about a dozen years. Before this it was covered with trees of twelve inches diameter, and round the base was an excavation of five feet depth and width, from whence the earth had been taken of which the hillock was formed.[19]

Then he gave the most minute, dispassionate, and objective descriptions of his findings. He related that he "first dug superficially in several parts of it, and came to collections of human bones, at different depths, from six inches to three feet below the surface." He found the bones positioned "in the utmost confusion, some vertical, some oblique, some horizontal, and directed to every point of the compass, entangled, and held together in clusters by the earth." Jefferson noted which bones were greatest in number and which seemed to be missing, the unusual order and juxtapositioning of various parts of the skeletons, which bones were fragile and which appeared to hold up well, what the "sculls" and the teeth and the ribs told about the age of the corpse.

Jefferson's next step was to introduce an element to archaeological investigation that preceded established practice by a hundred years: the use of stratigraphy. By this method, a calendar is developed by examining the various strata or layers in an archaeological investigation, the more recent relics being in the uppermost strata, the more ancient in the lower strata. Geologists made the earliest use of this technique following the publication of William Smith's *Strata Identified by Organized Fossils* in 1816. Jefferson, however, was the first to apply it deliberately to archaeology.[20]

Describing the Rivanna excavation, Jefferson wrote that he "proceeded then to make a perpendicular cut through the body of the barrow, that I might examine its internal structure. This passed about three feet from its center, was opened to the former surface of the earth, and was wide enough for a man to walk through and examine its sides."[21] By making this incision he was able to conduct a scientific observation: "At the bottom, that is, on the level of the circumjacent plain, I found bones; above these a few stones, brought from a cliff a quarter of a mile off, and from the river one-eighth of a mile off; then a large interval of earth, then a stratum of bones, and so on. At one end of the section were four strata of bones plainly distinguishable; at the other, three; the strata in one part not ranging with those in another. The bones nearest the surface were least decayed." He concluded then that the mound "has derived both origin and growth from the accustomary collection of bones, and deposition of them together; that the first collection had been deposited on the common surface of the earth, a few stones put over it, and then a covering of earth, that the second had been laid on this, had covered more or less of it in proportion to the number of bones, and was then also covered with earth; and so on."[22]

By this simple process, Jefferson introduced the foremost methodology of archaeologists today,[23] and his analysis of the bones went even further than merely establishing chronology:

No holes were discovered in any of them, as if made with bullets, arrows, or other weapons. I conjectured that in this barrow might have been a thousand skeletons. Every one will readily seize the circumstances above related, which militate against the opinion, that it covered the bones only of persons fallen in battle; and against the tradition also, which would make it the common sepulchre of a town, in which the bodies were placed upright, and touching each other. ... The following are the particular circumstances which give it this aspect. 1. The number of bones. 2. Their confused position. 3. Their being in different strata. 4. The strata in one part having no correspondence with those in another. 5. The different states of decay in these strata, which seem to indicate a difference in the time of inhumation. 6. The existence of infant bones among them.[24]

In a recent investigation of the Rapidan Mound, a site similar to the Rivanna location, Jeffrey Hantman, a professor of anthropology at the

University of Virginia, estimated that it contained between 1,000 and 1,500 people and that "on so many other points…it is quite remarkable how well Jefferson's interpretations hold up in the late twentieth century. His reading of the stratigraphy of the mound has been well supported by excavations at other mounds in Virginia."[25]

The importance of Jefferson's archaeological investigations lies both in the introduction of precise, deliberate, and replicable scientific methodology in investigation and in the change of focus from the collection of artifacts to gaining an understanding of the past. Jefferson's initial investigations were likely motivated not only by intellectual curiosity, but also by a desire to advance his country's goals and protect its reputation.

Jefferson continued to be interested in the history of the Indians and kept abreast of the latest news. In the 1780s, General Samuel Parsons made detailed maps of the earthwork discovered on the Muskingum River near Marietta and reported his finding to Ezra Stiles, who passed the information along to Jefferson. On July 8, 1790, an old acquaintance, Harry Innes, sent Jefferson information from the West, including "an image carved in stone of a naked woman kneeling…and a plan of old fortifications—which I have viewed & which are accurately laid down; from the great number which are discovered in this Western Country."[26]

Southern mounds received attention with the publication of William Bartram's *Travels Through North and South Carolina* in 1791, and the American Philosophical Society published Major Heart's accounts of multiple Indian mounds and fortifications in Ohio in 1793. Indeed, in 1797, the Committee on History of the American Philosophical Society, of which Jefferson was a member, articulated a desire "to obtain accurate plans, drawings and description of whatever is interesting…and especially of ancient fortification, Tumuli, and other Indian works of art, ascertaining the materials composing them, their contents, the purposes for which they were designed, &c."[27]

In 1803, Jefferson instructed Meriwether Lewis on the eve of his journey west to include information about the Indian nations and their monuments. But Jefferson did not seem to be aware of the full extent of the Indian remains until he received the report from Henry Brackenridge, to whom he responded, "I have read with pleasure the account it gives of the antient mounds & fortifications in the Western Country. I never before had an idea that they were so numerous."[28]

The study of "antient monuments" gave an insight into the antiquity of the native races, and the study of their religion, customs, relationships, and languages would provide further evidence of their origin. In many ways anthropology, ethnography, ethnogeny, and comparative linguistics arose in the new republic as a "patriotic reflex," providing erudite refutation of European charges of New World degeneracy and the polygenistic nature of the Indian.

Anthropology, Ethnology, Ethnogeny, and Comparative Linguistics

Drawing on multiple disciplines, Jefferson sought to refute the opinions of the Comte de Buffon and his allies in a logical and commonsensical way, using scientific and empirical proofs. The claim that climate adversely affected the size and variety of animals was discounted effectively by the simple expedient of comparing measurements of the size and weight of various species on each continent. The diversity and wholesomeness of vegetation could be likewise documented. But to counter the claims of physical, moral, and mental degeneracy of Native Americans, even to the point of naming them a separate species, was not such a straightforward business. In order to prove the physical, mental, and moral equality of Native Americans, and by extension those who migrate to America, it would be necessary to examine the customs, religions, and governments of the Indian tribes; in order to prove that all races derived from a common ancestor, and thereby demonstrate that Indians were not genetically inferior, it would be necessary to examine the origins of the indigenous races.

This required Jefferson to venture into the nascent disciplines of anthropology, which examines the physiology and psychology of humankind; ethnology, which deals with races, peoples, and their distinctive characteristics; and ethnogeny, the branch of ethnology that examines the origins of races.[29] Natural philosophers had long assumed that, in the absence of written records, the best proof of the relationship of one people to another was a comparison of their manners, morals, and society.

In 1786, Jefferson met John Ledyard in Paris, a young man he described as "of genius, of some science, and of fearless courage and enterprise." Jefferson suggested he make a voyage "by passing thro St Petersburg to Kamschatka" and from there obtain passage to America with a view "of exploring the Western coast."[30] Ledyard eagerly accepted the challenge and was within two hundred miles of his goal when he was arrested on the orders of the Empress Catherine and was forcibly returned to Poland. Nevertheless, a keen observer, Ledyard had been instructed by Jefferson to be on the lookout for evidence to counter Buffon's charges concerning Native Americans. Ledyard concluded that by "Customs, traditions and history" he was convinced of the "common origin" of the American Indian and the Asian, that "all the people you call red people on the continent of America and on the continents of Europe and Asia are all one people by whatever names distinguished and that the best general one would be *Tartar*....I suspect that *all* red people are of one family. I am satisfied myself that America was peopled from Asia and had some if not all its animals from thence."[31] But Jefferson viewed the evidence as coincidental rather than conclusive.

Some of the earliest students of Indian culture were Jesuit priests, and Father Joseph-François Lafitau was among the most prominent. In his 1724 book *Moeurs des sauvages Ameriqains*, which Jefferson owned, Lafitau relied on both personal experience and reports from fellow priests. He wrote in detail about religion, political government, marriage, and education; about occupations of both men and women; and about warfare, trade, and social issues among the Indians.[32] He described the matrilineal clan structure, the status of the chiefs and councils, and the role of women in society. He also drew comparisons between the social and political structures of the Mohawks and the Greeks and Romans. In *The History of the American Indian*, John Adair claimed that the Indians descended from the Hebrews and came to this conclusion by comparing the laws, rites, customs, priests, prophets, fasts, and festivals and the fact that "they all spoke Hebrew."[33] Jefferson dismissed Adair's notion as farfetched and he noted that Lafitau "selects ... all the facts and adopts all the falsehoods which favor this theory. ...He resided five years among the northern Indians, as a Missionary, but collects his matter much more from the writings of others than from his own observation."[34]

Perhaps the most credible of these early ethnographers was Jefferson's

friend and correspondent Constantin
François Chasseboeuf Volney. Early in
his life he decided to commit himself
to "l'etude des peoples," that is to say,
the comparative study of different national, ethnic, and religious groups.
For his first project, he took a boat to
Cairo, entered a Coptic monastery to
learn Arabic, and then set out on a
three-year tour of the cities, towns, and
Bedouin encampments of Egypt and
Syria.[35] On his return to Paris, he published *Voyage en Syrie et en Egypt, pen-*

*Constantine François Volney, Count
of Chasseboeuf,* by Gilbert Stuart
(ca. 1795).
*Courtesy of the Pennsylvania Academy of
the Fine Arts, Philadelphia. Gift of
Thomas Bayard.*

dant les annees 1783, 1784 et 1785, which examined all aspects of the
people he encountered, from agriculture and commerce to religion and
traits of character.[36]

In 1796, Volney visited Jefferson at Monticello in preparation for a
similar study among Native Americans. He journeyed west and reached
Indian settlements on the Wabash but abandoned his journey due to the
lawlessness of the country and the inhospitable treatment of strangers.[37]
Nevertheless, he devised a new technique in the field of anthropology
by conducting in-depth interviews with the chief of the Miami Indians,
Little Turtle. Much like a twenty-first-century ethnographer, he obtained
an extensive vocabulary and covered a
broad array of topics, from clothing
and child-rearing to tribal traditions of
racial origin.[38] Volney's participation
in Napoleon's premier scientific foundation, the *Institut National*, may have
helped establish its exacting requirements for anthropological studies,
which included, as Anthony F. C. Wallace has noted, "prolonged residence,
fluency in the alien language, and the
systematic observation according to a
predetermined set of standard cate-

Chief Little Turtle.
Courtesy of the Ohio Historical Society.

gories that would permit comparison and eventual generalization."[39] Jefferson's instructions to Meriwether Lewis may well have been based, in part, on Volney's novel approach to field work.

John Adams, with pointed candor, told Jefferson that his inquiries into the origins of Indians were a waste of time: "Whether serpents' teeth were sown here and sprang up men; whether men and women dropped from clouds upon this Atlantic Island; whether the Almighty created them here, or whether they emigrated from Europe, are questions of no moment to the present or future happiness of man."[40] By contrast, Albert Gallatin, Jefferson's secretary of the treasury and constant correspondent, saw great value in understanding the origins and mores of Native American groups, although his views were not always entirely charitable. In his *A Synopsis of the Indian Tribes within the United States East of the Rocky Mountains, and in the British and Russian Possessions in North America*, published a decade after Jefferson's death, Gallatin wrote that the Plains Indians who practiced agriculture were gentle and honorable, those who relied on hunting were indolent and improvident, and those who lived in game-scarce woodlands "were ferocious in warfare and vicious in torture." He asserted that the Iroquois "conquered only to destroy and had killed more Indians than the Europeans."[41]

Jefferson wrote to André Michaux a decade before the Lewis and Clark Expedition that "Sundry persons" had "subscribed certain sums of money for your encouragement to explore the country along the Missouri, & thence Westwardly to the Pacific ocean."[42] Among the matters of particular interest to Jefferson and other members of the American Philosophical Society was information relating to the aborigines, specifically "the names numbers, & dwellings of the inhabitants, and such particularities as you can learn of their history, connection with each other, languages, manners, state of society & of the arts & commerce among them."[43] The anthropological data he wanted Meriwether Lewis to collect was an expanded and more refined version of Michaux's charge, perhaps due to the influence and suggestions of Volney and Gallatin. In respect to the Indian nations, Jefferson wrote to Lewis:

The commerce which may be carried on with the people inhabiting the line you will pursue, renders a knolege of those people important. You will therefore endeavour to make yourself acquainted [with] as far as a diligent pursuit of your journey shall admit, with the names of the nations & their numbers; the extent & limits of their possessions; their relations with other tribes of nations; their language, traditions, monuments; their ordinary occupations in agriculture, fishing, hunting, war, arts & the implements for these; their food, clothing, & domestic accomodations; the diseases prevalent among them, & the remedies they use; moral & physical circumstances which distinguish them from the tribes we know; peculiarities in their laws, customs & dispositions; and articles of commerce they may need or furnish & to what extent. And considering the interest which every nation has in extending & strengthening the authority of reason & justice among the people around them, it will be useful to acquire what knolege you can of the state of morality, religion, & information among them; as it may better enable those who may endeavor to civilize & instruct them, to adapt their measures to the existing notions & practices of those on whom they are to operate.[44]

While ethnographic information was obviously valuable to a nation anticipating westward expansion in terms of political, economic, and military strategies, the question of the origin of Native Americans could still only be answered convincingly by a more concrete and definitive methodology. And Jefferson believed that the most incontrovertible evidence of the universal origin of man, which in turn would debunk the theories of continental degeneracy, would derive from a comparison of languages: "A knolege of their several languages would be the most certain evidence of their derivation which could be produced. In fact, it is the best proof of the affinity of nations which can ever be referred to."[45]

Comparative Linguistics

Enlightenment thinkers followed the Renaissance belief that the most eloquent and perfect language is observed in ancient European writings, specifically Greek and Latin texts. In 1786, Sir William Jones proclaimed at the meeting of the Asiatic Society of Bengal that "the Sanskrit language, whatever be its antiquity, is of wonderful structure; more perfect than the Greek; more copious than the Latin, and more exquisitely fine than either, yet bearing to both of them a stronger affinity ... than could possibly have been produced by accident; so strong indeed, that no philologer could examine all three, without believing them to have sprung from some common source."[46] With this pronouncement and its implication that the languages of Europe had derived from those of Asia, long-established theories of linguistic purity and superiority were shattered. Edward Gray, in *New World Babel*, asserted, "The significance of this statement cannot be overestimated. It rested on an empirical demonstration of the cultural links between East and West."[47]

The Reverend Nicholas Collin quickly picked up the thread that linked America by linguistic affinity to Europe by proposing that even the languages "of illiterate modern nations merit great attention...for some scalping heroes of America may be kinsmen of Alexander, Caesar, and the proudest conquerors of Europe."[48] John Adams, with a *mente mutata*, would later encourage Stephen Du Ponceau of the American Philosophical Society to preserve the records of native languages against the designs and intrusions of "the self-interested and corrupt who would write history with regard for only their own interests."[49] Only by preserving linguistic artifacts could objective, empirical knowledge be obtained, and only through empirical knowledge could the skeptical be convinced.

The concept of divining the truth about the heritage of Indians through etymological approaches was not new; Hugo Grotius advocated such a strategy as early as 1625 in his work *De Origine Gentium Americanarum*.[50] Nonetheless, Jefferson was clearly a pioneer in recognizing the value of collecting standardized vocabulary lists for comparing Indian languages.[51] His draft for *Notes on the State of Virginia* predated the publications of other studies in comparative linguistics of the era: Peter Pallas' *Linguatum totius orbis Comparativa Vocabularia* (1781), Benjamin Smith

Barton's *New Views on the Origins and Tribes of America* (1798), and Adelung and Vater's *Mithridates* (1806–1817).

In the plan outlined in *Notes on the State of Virginia*, Jefferson proposed securing the records of Indian literature and, at least, the general rudiments of Indian languages before they were lost to posterity. "Were vocabularies formed of all the languages spoken in North and South America, preserving their appellations of the most common objects in nature, of those that must be present to every nation barbarous or civilized, with the inflections of their nouns and verbs, their principles of regimen and concord, and these deposited in public libraries, it would furnish opportunities to those skilled in the languages of the old world to compare them with these, now, or at a future time, and hence to construct the best evidence of the derivation of the human race."[52]

Jefferson found a helpful collaborator in an old acquaintance from the Revolutionary times, Benjamin Hawkins,[53] who lived in Indian territories for many years. As early as 1786, Jefferson told Hawkins that he would gather Indian vocabularies and "shall take care so to dispose of what I collect thereon as that it shall not be lost."[54] For his part, Hawkins sent what vocabularies he could either write down himself or gather information from travelers who visited the native tribes. By 1800, Jefferson had a sizeable collection of the manuscripts and, in a state of precognition and anxiety, wrote Hawkins: "I have long believed we can never get any information of the antient history of the Indians, of their descent & filiation, but from a knolege & comparative view of their languages. I have, therefore, never failed to avail myself of any opportunity which offered of getting their vocabularies. I have now made up a large collection, and afraid to risk it any longer, lest by some accident it might be lost, I am about to print it."[55]

Jefferson began his compilations in earnest after his return from France and became convinced of the necessity of committing the vocabularies to paper after visiting a community of Unquachog Indians on Long Island. There he discovered that only three elderly women could still speak the language.[56] This experience seems to have compelled Jefferson to establish a careful collation of words common to all languages, grouping terms for body parts, time, opposites, foods, animals, natural phenomena, weather, and kinship. He gathered the names and vocabularies of twenty-two Indian tribes,[57] and before the Lewis and Clark Expedition, these were compiled in a document of some thirty pages titled "Manuscript Comparative Vocabulary of Several Indian Languages."[58]

By 1809, Jefferson had collected a list of approximately 250 words in as many as fifty Indian languages and was preparing to collate the lists with the recent works of Peter Pallas and J. S. Vater. By comparing his collection and Pallas' work of Russian etymological variations, he found seventy-three words in common, which would have enabled a study of the relationship between the Tartar dialects and the Indian languages. Indeed, at the beginning of his inquiries into the "filiations" of languages, he was of the opinion that the roots, or radices, of the Indian words were of separate origin, and therefore "a greater number of those radical changes of language having taken place among the red men of America, proves them of greater antiquity than those of Asia."[59] From this hypothesis, Jefferson judged that the Indians had originally migrated to Asia rather than from Asia. But the definitive works of Benjamin Barton Smith demonstrated that all American languages could "be referred to one great stock, which I call the language of the Lenni-Lennape or Delawares."[60] This combined with Sir William Jones' discovery of the lineage of Greek and Latin from Sanskrit seems to have convinced Jefferson that the Indians did migrate across the Bering Straits and that there might indeed be a common heritage of man.

Jefferson had expressed concerns about keeping the vocabularies safe and intended to publish them during his presidency. He had "now been thirty years availing myself of every opportunity of procuring Indian vocabularies to the same set of words: my opportunities were probably better than will ever occur again to any person having the same desire." He continued that he had even gone so far as to have "collected about 50. and had digested most of them into collateral columns and meant to have printed them the last year of my stay in Washington. but not having yet digested Capt Lewis's collection, nor having leisure then to do it, I put it off till I should return home."[61] It was on the trip back to Monticello that the "irreparable misfortune" occurred.

> the whole, as well digest as originals were packed in a
> trunk of stationary & sent round by water with about

English	sister	husband	wife
French	soeur	mari	femme
Delaware	douuiina	uihumuk	nihouushan
Unami	nchees-mus	we-ki-mat	noch-au-schum-mal
Monse	nchees-mas	we-chi-an	un-wal
Chippewa	dzhi-meh	na-peem	wi-wan
Knisteneaux	ne miss	ni nap pem	. . . . .
Algonquin	nimisain	ni na bem	. . . . .
Tawa	schi-meh	na-peem	wi-won
Shawanee	si-me-sa tolemah	ki-la-wo-schi-an wefsigue	wi-wa-li newah
Nanticoke	nimps.neighsum nih-simps	nups-sch!soh! weh-sic	nee-ee-wah! wi-uch
Mohiccon	na-tom-baso ni.ta-pa-su	n-push wach-ier	we-na-so wi-wa
...chog	keessums	ks-hamps	kee-us
Oneida	oanphiadanusch	tiaganeiti	nailo-oh
Cayuga	. . . . .		
Onondaga	akzia	. . . . .	
Miame	shema akoshimomah	pemah anapimeemah	wiwah ueomah
Cherokee	inketoh anketo aenkataugh	aguotul.te.ch.ootalleeh aguotellee	cheyapuh.aguotalleeh aguotellee
Chickasaw	nuckfis	e.sipp.pe.	ow,wau,uh.
Choctaw	inteape aimteke	e.hultuck.	take,cheh.takeche
Creek	e.choo.se	e.he	e.high.wau.
Tuscarora	. . . . .	. . . . .	. . . . .
Chetimacha	hichekithiepa	hichehase	hiche kithia
Atacapa	penn	iol	nichib

Jefferson's Indian vocabularies.
Courtesy of the American Philosophical Society.

Archaeology, Anthropology, Ethnology, and Comparative Linguistics

30. other packages of my effects from Washington, and while ascending James river, this package, on account of it's weight & presumed precious contents, was singled out & stolen. the thief being disappointed on opening it, threw into the river all it's contents of which he thought he could make no use. among these were the whole of the vocabularies. some leaves floated ashore & were found in the mud; but these were very few, & so defaced by mud & water that no general use can ever be made of them.[62]

3

Paleontology

*Being informed you have retired from Public Business and
returned to your former residence in Albemarle, and observ-
ing by your Notes your very curious desire for Examining
into the antiquity of our Country, I thought the Bones of a
Tremendious Animal of the Clawed kind lately found ...
might afford you some amusement, have therefore procured
you such as were saved.*
—JOHN STUART TO THOMAS JEFFERSON,
APRIL 11, 1796

Although Jefferson had been alerted to information concerning animals of tremendous size and antiquity, John Stuart's news must have
fired his imagination both with scientific possibilities and the opportunities to deal resounding blows to Buffon's theory of natural degeneracy
in America. Jefferson has been called the "Father of American Paleontology."[1] Although some have questioned this distinction,[2] none can refute the tremendous contributions Jefferson made to this nascent field of
science. As in archaeology, Thomas Jefferson was not the first to study the
subject, but he introduced an element of scientific method and utility
that elevated the field from the realm of curious inquiry to that of a serious discipline.

The history of collecting and examining fossils surely extends into pre-Columbian times. In 1519, a captain in the army of Cortez, Bernal Diaz del Castillo, reported that the Tlascalan Indians had brought pieces of "bones of great size, but much consumed by time. ...We were astonished at these remains."[3] Among these was a thigh-bone, about which the captain wrote "[It] was of my height, though I am as tall as the generality of men."[4] The Tlascalans told the story handed down from their ancestors that "in former times the country was inhabited by men and women of great stature, and wicked manners, whom their ancestors at length extirpated"[5] and they brought forth the fossils as evidence.

Interest in paleontological matters also emerged in northern America. In 1636, Samuel Maverick reported the discovery of fossils and antediluvian shells found in Virginia; in 1686, John Banister presented prehistoric bones and teeth to an English traveler; in 1706, Governor Dudley of New York reported to Cotton Mather that "two honest Dutchmen" had brought to him "a certain tooth, accompanied by some other pieces of bone,"[6] which he surmised were of ancient origin. Mather responded that in 1705 a giant tooth "four pounds and three quarters" in weight and a thigh-bone "seventeen feet long" were found in Albany. Mather's published report, which appeared in *Philosophical Transactions* in 1714, may well be the first printed description of such fossils in North America.[7] According to historian George Simpson, the first "technical identification of an American fossil vertebrate" was made by African slaves, as indicated by this account published in 1743 by natural historian Mark Catesby:

> All parts of *Virginia*, at the distance of Sixty Miles, or more, [from the sea] abound in Fossil Shells of various Kinds, which in Stratums lie imbedded a great Depth in the Earth, in the Banks of the Rivers and other Places, among which are frequently found the *Vertibras*, and other Bones of Sea Animals. At a plane in *Carolina* called *Strono*, was dug out of the Earth three or four teeth of a large animal, which, by the concurring Opinion of all the *Negroes*, native *Africans*, that saw them, were grinders of an Elephant, and in my

Opinion they could be no other; I having seen some of the like that are brought from *Africa*.[8]

In 1739, Charles le Moyne, Baron de Longueuil, led an expedition from Montreal to New Orleans. During his journey he came upon a marsh in what is now Kentucky, where he found large bones and teeth that appeared to be those of an elephant. The site would later be known as Big Bone Lick. He took these remains, "including a tusk, a femur, and at least three molars,"[9] to New Orleans. From there the fossils were sent to Paris and placed in the King's Bureau of Curiosities, the Cabinet du Roi, then transferred to the Jardin des Plantes and put into the care of Georges Cuvier. These remains became a popular object of study, and Buffon's protégé, Louis Jean Marie Daubenton, pronounced in 1762 that "the tusk and femur to be those of an elephant and the grinders those of a hippopotamus."[10]

In 1751, Christopher Gist was given two mastodon teeth by Robert Smith, one of which was sent to London. Several British and French expeditions made their way to the marsh during the 1750s, and word began to reach natural historians concerning the "Wonderfull Discoveries Near the Ohio."[11]

James Wright wrote to Quaker botanist John Bartram in 1762 that "pursuant to thy request" he had inquired about the bones of Big Bone Lick and had been told that "the remains of 5 Entire Sceletons, with their heads all pointing towards Each other" had been found with heads so large that a "Man Could but Just Grasp in Both his Arms." The shoulder socket was "equal in Size to a large bowl," and "the thigh bone when broke asunder, would admit of a little boy's Creeping into it."[12] The explorers had also reported that the specimens had horns "10 to 12 feet long" and "Judged the Creature[s] when alive to have been the Size of a Small house."[13] Wright learned that, according to native American tradition, "such mighty Creatures, once frequented the Savannahs, that there were men of a size proportional to them, who used to kill them and tye them in Their Noppusses" and that God had "kill'd these last 5" by "lightening" "that they should not hurt the Present race of Indians."[14]

Among the more famous gatherers of fossils from Big Bone Lick was George Croghan, who was sent in 1765 to mediate with the Indians on behalf of the British authorities. When he arrived, he found "vast quantities of these bones lying five or six feet under ground" including "two tusks over six feet long."[15] Captain Croghan's stay at Big Bone Lick was abruptly ended by an attack of hostile Indians, from whom he "got the stroke of a Hatchet on the Head" but that his "skull being pretty thick, the hatchet could not enter."[16] Croghan progressed from this point first to New Orleans then to New York, from which city he dispatched fossil samples to Benjamin Franklin and to Lord Shelburne in London. Franklin received five tusks, a vertebra, and three molars. In 1767, Franklin gratefully acknowledged receipt of the specimens and noted that the tusks agreed "with those of the African and Asiatic elephant. ... But the grinders differ, being full of knobs, like the grinders of a carnivorous animal."[17]

The English naturalist William Hunter studied Croghan's collection in London and reported to the Royal Society on February 25, 1768, that the *incognitum* of America was probably the same as the "Mammouth of Siberia," and in former times its habitat was global. He added that if this mammal were carnivorous, "as men we cannot but thank heaven that its whole generation is probably extinct."[18]

For his part, Jefferson thought the process of extinction, while not impossible, ran against the dictates of nature. He wrote to John Stuart, "I cannot however help believing that this animal as well as the Mammoth are still existing. The annihilation of any species of existence is so unexampled in any parts of the economy of nature which we see, that the probabilities against such annihilation are stronger than those for it."[19]

Dr. Christian Michaelis, a graduate of the University of Strasburg who had studied with both John Hunter and Sir John Pringle, came to America in 1779 as a Hessian physician attached to British forces. Since his duties were not excessive in New York, he was encouraged to cultivate his abilities in natural history by investigating the mysteries of the mastodons.

In 1780, the Reverend Robert Annan made a discovery of fossils on his farm near Walkill in Orange County, New York. Michaelis requested help from General George Washington in excavating the Annan site and "Washington provided a dozen men, with tools and wagons; but the unremitting rains so flooded the swamp that Michaelis had to stop."[20] Nevertheless, he obtained some bones from the Annan site which he subsequently placed in the museum at Cassel. Michaelis continued his interest in the collection of fossils and intended to make a foray into Ohio himself but was dissuaded by an Indian uprising in the area.

Michaelis, having heard of Dr. Morgan's collection of fossils in Philadelphia, visited the good doctor when he arrived in that city. He was shocked to find the fossils still covered in mud fifteen years after their discovery. He convinced Morgan to allow Charles Willson Peale, a prominent Philadelphia artist and natural scientist, to make drawings of his fossils and conveyed them to Peale's studio. Peale's brother-in-law, Colonel Nathaniel Ramsey," upon seeing them, exclaimed that he would willingly travel twenty miles to see such an interesting collection, and he was sure that other persons would, like himself, rather see such amazing curiosities of nature than any paintings at all. …The result was that Charles Willson Peale's American Museum derived its inspiration from a box of ancient mastodon's bones, collected on the Ohio by an Indian trader, owned by a well-known Philadelphia physician, [and] drawn by an eminent American portrait painter for a young German army doctor."[21]

In January 1780, the American Philosophical Society announced the election of new members Thomas Jefferson, General George Washington, and Monsieur Marbois of the Embassy of France. Marbois' request for precise information concerning the individual states presented Jefferson not only with the perfect opportunity not only for organizing his various notes on Virginia into a convenient framework but also for addressing Buffon's assertions that New World flora and fauna were, by nature, smaller, weaker, and generally inferior to those of the Old World. Jefferson knew this charge was absurd and scientifically insupportable. In his *Notes on the State of Virginia*, he used a precise survey to compare the size and weight of various animals indigenous to both continents to refute Buffon's allegations objectively. But the subject of the mastodons presented an area in which the New World not only achieved parity with the Old World, but actually surpassed anything Europe had to offer. Jefferson at this time must also have been cognizant of the reports of fossil bones of "Tremendous" size from Franklin, Washington, and Rittenhouse. He expressed his ambition to locate and study these relics and wrote to James Steptoe in 1782, "A specimen of each of the several series

NOTES on the ſtate of VIRGINIA;
written in the year 1781, ſomewhat cor-
rected and enlarged in the winter of 1782,
for the uſe of a Foreigner of diſtinction, in
anſwer to certain queries propoſed by him
reſpecting

MDCCLXXXII.

Jefferson's *Notes on the State of Virginia.*
Courtesy of the American Philosophical Society.

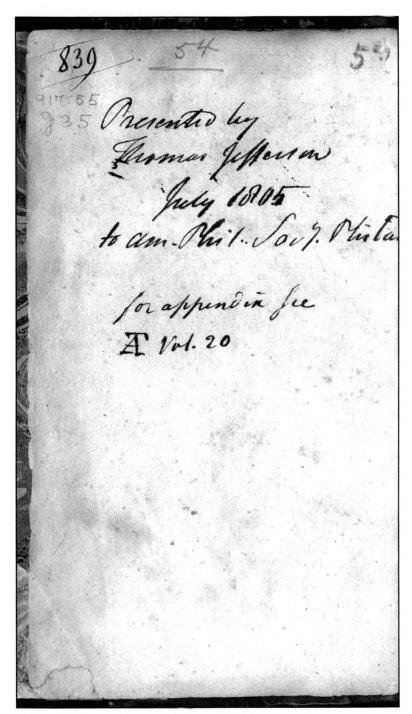

Jefferson's *Notes on the State of Virginia*, presentation copy.
Courtesy of the American Philosophical Society.

of bones now to be found, is to me the most desirable object in natural history."[22]

Having completed his diplomatic duties in France, Jefferson received the following intelligence from John Stuart at Monticello:

> observing by your Notes your very curious desire for Examining into the antiquitys of our Country, I thought the Bones of a Tremendous Animal of the Clawed kind lately found in a Cave ... might afford you some amusement, have therefore procured you such as were saved, (for before I was informed of them they were chiefly lossed). ...I do not remembered to have seen any account in the History of our Country, or any other, which was probabelly of the Lion kind; I am induced to think so from a perfect figure of that animal carved upon a rock near the confluence of the Great Kenawha, which appears to me to have been done many centurys ago.[23]

Jefferson, who piled proof upon proof against Buffon's theory, often at great personal expense, quickly digested the import of the letter. He wrote to John Stuart's cousin, "the bones are too extraordinary in themselves, and too victorious an evidence against the pretended degeneracy of animal nature in our continent, not to excite the strongest desire to push the enquiry after all other remains of the same animal which any industry can recover for us."[24] The fossilized remains offered a dramatic rebuttal to Buffon's theory, but even more promising was new information that gave fervent hope that the species might yet be alive. John Stuart wrote in July 1796, "I have never heared of any bones of this kind any where before; but an account I had from two persons in the year 1769 when I first come to this Country (then inhabited only by a few Hunters) induces me to think that such a Creature yet exists."[25] Conventional wisdom held that dogs and horses are acutely alert to supernatural dangers. What Stuart related confirmed his suspicions concerning the prehistoric beast:

George Wilson, and John Davis, informed they were lying on the cheat River some time in the year 1765 in the nighttime something approached their Camp with astonishing roaring and very much alarmed them, their dogs srunk and lay down at their feet refuseing to bark, as it drew nerer its cry became in their Opinion as loud as thunder, and the Stomping seemed to make the ground shake, the darkness of the night prevented their seeing their enemy tho they stood long with their arms to defend themselves.[26]

Jefferson must have related this incident to Philip Turpin who, in turn, confirmed John Stuart's intuition. He repeated an account of the Moors' experiences with lions, which he had read in the *Gentleman's & London Magazine* of 1783. He noted that when Moorish hunting parties encounter lions, "their Horses, though famous for their swiftness, are seiz'd with so strong a terror, that they become motionless, and that the Dogs, not less timid, keep creeping to the feet of their master, or of his horse."[27]

Before the second letter from John Stuart arrived, Jefferson had already written to David Rittenhouse in Philadelphia that bones had been found "of an animal of the family of lion, tiger, panther &c. but as preeminent over the lion in size as the Mammoth is over the elephant."[28] Jefferson detailed the size of the bones in his possession and proposed, "It's bulk entitles it to give our animal the name of the Great-claw or Megalonyx."[29] Since David Rittenhouse died before the arrival of Jefferson's letter, it was passed on to Rittenhouse's nephew, Benjamin Smith Barton, by Rittenhouse's widow.[30] Barton informed Jefferson, "The 4th vol. of the *Transactions* of our Philosophical Society is now in press. About 150 pages are printed off. Your account of the bones lately discovered, will be very acceptable to us."[31]

Jefferson replied belatedly to Barton in October that he had been waiting "in daily expectation of recieving some other bones of the newly discovered animal which would have enabled me to write to you more satisfactorily."[32] He was hoping to obtain a thigh-bone, which would have allowed a more exact calculation of the creature's height than an estimation by "ex pede Herculem." Even without a thigh-bone, the available evidence indicated the Megalonyx was indeed "the most tremendous of animals."[33] Barton informed Jefferson that it would be at least two months before the fourth volume of the *Transactions* would be published, and there was still time to send the article.

Upon his election as both vice president of the United States and as president of the American Philosophical Society, Jefferson received a congratulatory note from his old friend Benjamin Rush. He responded to Rush, "I thank you too for your congratulations on the public call on me to undertake the 2d. office in the US. but still more from the justice you do me in viewing as I do the *escape* from the first. ...If I am to act however, a more tranquil and unoffending station could not be found for me, nor one so analogous to the dispositions of my mind. It will give me philosophical evenings in the winter and rural days in the summer."[34] Jefferson also sent an official letter of acceptance to the Secretaries of the American Philosophical Society, in which he describes his election as "the most flattering incident of my life, and that to which I am the most sensible." And with his accustomed modesty he added, "My satisfaction would be complete were it not for the consciousness that it is far beyond my titles."[35] In his letter to Rush, Jefferson announced both his hope that "the usual delays of publication of the society may admit the addition, to our new volume, of this interesting article" and his intention of being in Philadelphia in the first week of March.[36]

Within a fortnight Rush assured Jefferson that his article "will arrive time en'o to have a place in the volume of the transactions of the philosophical Society which is now in the press."[37] Rush drew a comparison between the erstwhile "tyrants of our forests" and the present day monarchs, which will be "extirpated from the face of the earth by a general insurrection of reason and Virtue" and that an "exhibition of crowns, Scepters and maces, like the claws and bones of extinct Animals, shall be necessary to prove to posterity, that such canibals ever existed."[38] And in one sentence, Rush makes clear his belief in the evolution of both political and biological systems.[39]

Jefferson had been working through January and into February to finish his "Memoir on the Megalonyx," and completed a copy dated February 10, 1797. On February 20, he left from Monticello for Philadelphia to assume office. He hoped to arrive in quick order and "under the shadow of the coach and unperceived to avoid any formal reception,"[40] but bad weather on the Chesapeake Bay and other circumstances kept him on the road for ten days. Arriving only two days before the inauguration, Jefferson could not avoid public fanfare. He was greeted by an artillery company's cannonade of salvos and banners proclaiming "Jefferson the Friend of the People."[41]

Jefferson took up residence, *pro tempore*, with the Madisons until he could procure lodgings of his own. In the intervening time between his arrival and his inauguration, he visited the bookstalls, as was his custom. He happened upon a recent edition of the *Monthly Magazine and British Register for 1796* containing an article that included an etching of a fossilized skeleton recently found in South America and "boldly labeled as belonging to a species hitherto unknown." The skeleton was mounted and housed in the Royal Cabinet of Natural History in Madrid.[42] The etching and the description of the skeleton must have been, at the same moment, both exhilarating and debilitating to Jefferson. It was the same creature as his Megalonyx, but it had been discovered and named the Megatherium before Jefferson's revelation, and, more alarming still, it was clear that it did not belong to the family "of lions, tygers, or panthers." As the eminent Jefferson scholar Julian Boyd wryly observed, "For millions of years the bones of the megalonyx and megatherium had lain undisturbed on separate continents. Now, within the space of a single week, they had collided on the streets of Philadelphia."[43]

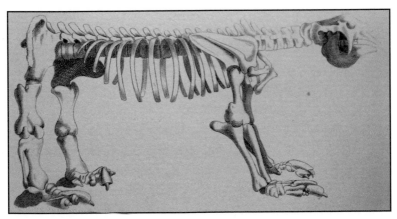

Bru's Megalonyx.
Thomas Jefferson Papers, 1796.

Jefferson immediately realized his error in identifying the Megalonyx as a member of the cat family.[44] In his inaugural address to the Philosophical Society, he acknowledged the *Monthly Magazine* article but maintained the distinction of names. He noted cautiously that the findings were preliminary and that final judgment should be suspended until all the information was assembled. However, there could have been little doubt in his mind that both skeletons belonged to the same species.

It is perhaps even more ironic that Jefferson had been in possession of the same information for nearly a decade. While he was lodged in the Hôtel de Langeac in Paris awaiting his departure for home, a letter arrived from William Carmichael, the American Charge d'Affairs in Madrid. It included an insert entitled "Description of the Megatherium," which detailed a "curious piece of anatomy" found near "the river luxan fourteen leagues from buenos aires in profound creck 10 yeards of heigtnes."[45] The remains were characterized as "almost calcinated and petrified" and likely belonging to the family of the largest quadrupeds, the elephant, hippopotamus, or rhinoceros.[46] The specifications of the skeleton listed weights and dimensions for the entire length and height of the creature and individual descriptors for the "head and vertebre, dorsales and lumbares, the right arm, the right leg and the sacra and innominata."[47] The unidentified writer of the enclosure concluded:

> In this skeleton were found almost all the bones which compose its structure. The Tusks and the extremity of the head, the snout are Wanting. And also the phalanges which compose the fourth finger of the posteriour feet. Parts of the ribs and other litle bones. …We expect the conclution of thte Whole skeleton, to have a better figure for this is a very imperfect one.[48]

Jefferson thanked Carmichael for the enclosure,[49] packed the papers away and, from that point in time, was oblivious to its existence. According to Julian Boyd, "Thus, all during 1796 they were within arm's reach in his notable library and personal archive at Monticello. Not once then, or apparently ever, did Jefferson remember them."[50]

Jefferson's presentation before the American Philosophical Society

Jefferson's revised notes on Megalonyx.
Courtesy of the Library of Congress.

aroused such interest among the members that a committee was established to promote research on American antiquities and natural history. Two excavation sites that commanded special excitement were Big Bone Lick in Kentucky and Orange and Ulster counties in New York.[51] Having been informed about a large find of fossils near Shawangunk in Ulster County by the Reverend Ezra Stiles,[52] Jefferson wrote to his friend Robert Livingston, who lived nearby, seeking information:

> I have heard of the discovery of some large bones, supposed to be of the mammoth, at about 30. or 40. miles

distance from you; and among the bones found, are said to be some of which we have never yet been able to procure. The 1st interesting question is, whether they are the bones of the mammoth? The 2d, what are the particular bones, and could I possibly procure them? The bones I am most anxious to obtain, are those of the head & feet, which are said to be among those found in your State, as also the ossa innominata, and the scapula. Others would also be interesting, though similar ones may be possessed, because they would show by their similarity that the set belong to the mammoth.[53]

In his reply, Livingston told Jefferson that when he first heard of the discovery, "I made some attempts to possess myself of them, but found they were a kind of common property the whole town having joined in diging for them till they were stoped by the autumnal rains."[54] Though Livingston despaired of obtaining any of the fossils, he was optimistic about their condition and their completeness: "They entertain well grounded hopes of discovering the whole skeleton since the bones are not, like all others that they have hitherto found in that country, placed within the vegetable mould, but are covered with a stratum of clay, so that being better sheltered from the air & water they are more perfectly preserved."[55] And like Jefferson, Livingston believed that the American incognitum clearly contradicted Buffon and other European naturalists who clung to his theory.[56]

The news of the find in Ulster County excited in Charles Willson Peale the hope of obtaining a complete skeleton of a mammoth for his museum in Philadelphia. Peale immediately grasped that the uniqueness and exotic nature of this find would bring fame and notoriety to his museum and wealth and reputation to his family. He rushed to the site of the discovery, the farm of John Masten, and, under the guise of only wanting to make some drawings, insinuated himself into the household of the old farmer. He would later write, "I did not give the least hint of my Intention to purchase, & liberty was readily granted me to make my drawings."[57] That evening Peale was invited to dinner by the Mastens, and the

Exhumation of the Mastodon by Charles Willson Peale.
Courtesy of the Maryland Historical Society.

eldest son asked him if he would like to buy the bones. After considerable haggling, Peale "offered 200 Drs. For those now collected and 100 Drs. at some other time when I could bear the expence."[58] The next day the farmer agreed to the terms, but upon seeing Peale's excitement, demanded also a double-barreled gun for his eldest son and gowns from New York for his daughters.[59]

With the showmanship of P. T. Barnum, Peale returned with his drawings, a huge thigh-bone, and his stories in tow, creating great excitement in their wake. He arranged for the bones to be transported to Philadelphia aboard the schooner *David*, and a large crowd greeted Peale and the bones in the harbor. *Kline's Carlisle Weekly Gazette* reported that Peale had obtained "bones of the great American animal commonly called the *Mammoth*" and planned to assemble "a complete skeleton for the Museum."[60]

On July 24, 1801, Peale made a presentation to the American Philosophical Society and requested $500 from the society to make a systematic search of the Ulster County area for complete skeletons. Finding the spot of previous discoveries inundated with water, Peale constructed an enormous water wheel to drain the excavation.[61] President Jefferson instructed the Secretary of the Navy, Robert Smith, to send support, a pump, and several tents to assist the effort.[62] This is the first documented record of American government intervention in the pursuit of science and may well have set a precedent.

Charles Willson Peale and his son, Rembrandt, accomplished this feat with dramatic flair. Rembrandt had a local blacksmith fabricate two long metal poles to probe the morass, Charles made a cinematic painting of the enterprise, sightseers and journalists from all over came to view the proceedings, and Peale assembled the disparate bones into an articulated and completed skeleton. All of this was accomplished within three months. The Peales had actually uncovered not one, but two mammoth skeletons; the first was kept at Peale's museum in Philadelphia, and the other went on a European tour with Rembrandt. As the skeletons were assembled, missing parts in one were replicated from parts in the other, and when the museum's specimen was completed, it stood eleven feet tall at the shoulder and was seventeen feet in length from the tips of the tusks to the end of the tail.[63]

Thus, Peale had taken a quantum leap from stuffing exotic birds to displaying an entire prehistoric skeleton, causing a greater sensation than even he had anticipated. The first display was opened to members of the American Philosophical Society on Christmas Eve, 1801. The next day, the addition to the museum, Mammoth Hall, was opened to the public for the additional charge of 50 cents. Handbills dramatically propounded the Shawnee legend of a thundering monster that roamed "ten thousand moons ago," and an actor dressed in native finery pranced through town with a trumpeter riding ahead to herald the astounding find. People flocked to the museum to see "the ninth wonder of the world!!!"[64] Few were disappointed. The whole city went mammoth crazy, which helped to discredit the condescending theories of the arrogant French academics.

In the process of freeing the bones from the swamp, Peale had made another discovery, which was just one link formed between the hunt for ancient animals and the emerging sciences of geology, mineralogy, and chemistry:

> All the Morasses where these Bones have been found,
> have marly bottoms. Bones found in the whitest shell-
> marle, are the most perfect, those parts found in bluish

marle, less so, and bones found in black marles, generally are in total decay.[65]

In December 1802, Jefferson consulted with the Spanish minister and the French legation's secretary about the desire of the United States to send an exploring party through their western territories for the purpose of collecting scientific data. A similar scheme had been proposed by the American Philosophical Society almost a decade before, with nearly the same instructions and a French naturalist, André Michaux, as the leader. The expedition failed, but the concept of the mission remained. This time Jefferson had personally selected a man of many talents and great bravery to head the Corps of Discovery, Meriwether Lewis. The French and Spanish agreed to allow the expedition to pass through their territories unmolested. Jefferson proposed the venture to Congress, which approved the operation by law on February 28, 1803.

Jefferson not only had the *auctoritas* of the office of president of the United States to back his expedition, but also the intellectual *gravitas* as president of the American Philosophical Society to provide the necessary scientific expertise and to give the venture the stamp of scientific legitimacy, allaying potential concerns of espionage and expansionism. Jefferson enlisted the aid of society members to train and equip the corps: Benjamin Smith Barton for botany, Caspar Wistar for zoology, Robert Patterson for astronomy, Benjamin Rush for medicine and physic, and Andrew Ellicott for surveying and cartography.[66]

He wanted Lewis to conduct scientific observations and to chart with accuracy the lands of the West;[67] take careful notes concerning potentially useful plants, animals, and minerals;[68] describe the nature and governance of various Indian tribes and engage in diplomatic exchanges with them;[69] and make meteorological surveys.[70] These were the ground rules for one of the greatest scientific fishing expeditions ever undertaken. And no one was disappointed with the results.

Lewis started the trip with a visit to Dr. William Goforth and a journey to Big Bone Lick, looking for a mastodon skull. The few fossils he found, Lewis sent from Natchez to the White House, and as often happened, they never arrived. Next Lewis set off for Louisville, where he was to meet Clark and the other twenty-nine members of the expedition.

Later Clark would undertake the same commission but with greater success. Over several weeks, he collected numerous samples from Big Bone Lick and sent them via New Orleans and Baltimore to the president.[71] Jefferson described the collection as "containing more than three hundred specimens," among which were "four pieces of head, four jawbones … three elephant tusks, one different from the others and of excessive size, being from nine to ten feet in length." He immediately informed Caspar Wistar of the find and summoned him to the White House. The bones were spread out in what would become popularly known as the "Mammoth Room," and Wistar was able to work with the items at his leisure from morning to night.[72]

Jefferson sent duplicate bones to Paris, where they were received with considerable enthusiasm. With the specimens, Cuvier was able to reconstruct two lost species, the *mastodon americanus* and the *elephans primigenius*.[73] In a letter to Charles Willson Peale, Jefferson wrote, "I have no doubt that the marked differences between the elephant & our colossal animal entitle him to a distinct appellation. one of those differences, & a striking one, is in the protuberances on the grinding surface of the teeth, somewhat in the shape of the mamma, mastos, or brest of a woman, which has induced Cuvier to call it the Mastodonte, or bubby-toothed."[74]

A more startling development concerning the ancient beast was revealed to Jefferson in a letter from Wistar. Even today the report has a surreal aspect.

The most interesting accounts of the Siberian Mammoth that have ever appeared have lately been published in the European Journals. They state that the entire Animal has been discovered at the mouth of the Lena River in the frozen sea. One of the Natives discovered it in a Mass of Ice at the mouth of the River & watched it for several Summers before it was disengaged from the Ice, at length…it was extricated from the Ice, & appeared with the Skin & all the Soft parts. The size of the Animal was 9 feet in heighth & 14 in length from the nose to the end of ye Caccysis…bone—He had a long mane on his neck &

bristles over the Skin with thick hair also—the tusks were about 9 feet long…the account of this very extraordinary fact is published by a physician of St. Petersburgh who was on the Spot & procured the sceleton.[75]

In 1808, General William Clark made a second shipment of mammoth bones to Washington, but they were lost in transit. Jefferson sought them out. He wrote to the harbor master of Georgetown that the vessel left New Orleans and put in at Havana, where the ship was "condemned as not sea-worthy." Jefferson suspected the shipment was left there.[76] Jefferson informed Clark, "what was done with my 3. boxes I have not learned. … the bones are in such a state of evanescence now as to render it important to save what we can of them. of those you had formerly sent me I reserved a very few for myself, got Doctr Wistar to select from the rest every piece which could be interesting to the Philosophical society, & sent the residue to the National institute of France."[77] Considering the specimens he had seen, Jefferson concluded from the "form & immense mass of their jaws" that the creature must have been "arboriverous" and that a "limb of a tree would be no more to him than a bough of a Cotton tree to a horse."[78]

Jefferson's contributions to paleontology manifested themselves in initial investigations and scientific applications to matters that were before thought of as curious parlor games for royalty and rich men. And from these new considerations arose other branches of science that were previously either disregarded or dismissed: geology, climatology, and chemistry. His royal cabinet was not located in the sanctum sanctorum of a gated castle but rather in a simple entrance hall open to all his fellow citizens.

A major portion of Jefferson's collections, through means both private and public, were given to the American Philosophical Society. With contributions not only from Jefferson, but also from Caspar Wistar and Benjamin Smith Barton, the society's collection grew to the point that in 1849 it was decided to disperse the collections to other institutions. Among them was the Academy of Natural Sciences of Philadelphia, where most of the fossils Jefferson collected for the society still reside.[79]

Of Jefferson's personal collection, a small part remains at Monticello, but a majority of the fossils, along with scientific instruments and other collections, was handed over by Thomas Jefferson Randolph in 1826 to the recently opened University of Virginia. No catalogue was made for the donations, and over time they became dispersed and interspersed throughout the University's departments. The location of these remains is still a mystery, although there is a persistent legend of a box labeled *Tom's Bones* latently lying somewhere on University property.

Silvio Bedini stated that although Jefferson was not the first to collect or study vertebrate fossils, he was the first in America to publish on the subject. Although he was not trained as a paleontologist (no one was at that time), and although his other occupations prevented him from conducting extensive field work, he religiously appointed others to search for him. Bedini further observed:

> Of considerable importance to the development of American vertebrate paleontology was his tenacious pursuit of fossil remains at considerable expenditure of his own funds, as well as his encouragement of the collection and study of fossil remains by others. In this manner he succeeded in promoting wide interest and support of the subject during its embryonic period.[80]

4

Social Architecture and Public Health

*I consider the common plan, followed in this country, but
not in others, of making one large and expensive building as
unfortunate erroneous. it is infinitely better to erect a small
and separate lodge for each professorship...joining these
lodges by...a covered walkway to give dry communication
between all the schools. The whole being arranged around an
open square of grass & trees would make it, what it should
be in fact, an academical village, instead of large & common den of noise, of filth, & of fetid air....I pray you par-
don me, if I have stepped aside into the province of counsel:
but much observation & reflection on these institutions have
long convinced me that the large & crouded buildings in
which youths are pent up, are equally unfriendly to health, to
study, to manners, moral & order.*

—THOMAS JEFFERSON TO THE TRUSTEES OF THE
LOTTERY FOR EAST TENNESSEE COLLEGE,
MAY 6, 1810

For Jefferson, the main tenets of the Scottish Enlightenment—scientific method, utility, and improvement—come together in no other place
so neatly as in the development of public architecture. Although Jefferson

railed against doctors with the same sarcasm and skepticism that Cicero heaped on the profession of augurs, he nevertheless took an early and abiding interest in medical issues. His greatest concern was in the area of infectious diseases, particularly smallpox, yellow fever, and the environments that promoted the diseases.

The scourge of smallpox bedeviled humankind for many centuries. A form of inoculation known as variolation was practiced as a preventative by the Chinese and the Africans from ancient times, and by the eighteenth century, the effectiveness of such treatments became known to the Byzantines and Ottomans. The Royal Society of London published favorable accounts of the smallpox vaccine by Emanuel Timoni of Constantinople and Jacobus Pylarini of Venice in its *Philosophical Transactions* in 1714. In April 1718, the first inoculation in England was performed on the daughter of Lady Mary Wortly Montagu, a prominent London socialite. The procedure, which induced a mild form of the disease when successful, soon became widely used both in British society and in the British armed forces.

Early American advocates of inoculation included Cotton Mather and Dr. Zabdiel Boylston. In May 1721, an outbreak of smallpox occurred in Boston, and about a month later, Dr. Boylston introduced the practice into the colonies by inoculating his own son and two slaves. By the end of the outbreak, he had inoculated 247 persons and was threatened with hanging for his efforts.[1] Fears about catching the disease and concerns about attempts to alter the plan of God precluded many colonists from taking the preventative steps.

In England, before Edward Jenner's safer cowpox-based vaccine was introduced in 1798, smallpox was responsible for an estimated 10 percent of all deaths in Britain, and a fourth of the population had been disfigured by the disease.[2] Jefferson likely discussed this affliction with his friends in the *partie quarree*, for Francis Fauquier and his brother were both members of the Royal Society.[3] Another figure associated with members of that group, Benjamin Franklin, had collaborated on a pamphlet promoting inoculation with distinguished London physician William Heberden in 1759.[4]

Describing an outbreak of smallpox in Boston, Franklin wrote, "At first endeavours were used to prevent its spreading, by removing the sick, or guarding the houses in which they were; and with the same view Inoculation was forbidden; but when it was found that these endeavours were fruitless, the distemper breaking out in different quarters of the town, and increasing, Inoculation was then permitted."[5] He noted that "the practice of Inoculation always divided the people into parties, some contending warmly for it, and the others against it."[6] Therefore the town magistrates ordered that "a strict and impartial inquiry be made by the constables of each ward" to determine the effectiveness of the inoculation process. The results were that 5,059 of those counted "had the Small-Pox in the common way," and of those, 452 died. By comparison, 1,974 were inoculated for the disease, and of these, 23 died.[7] Proponents of inoculation claimed that the deaths occurred in weak children, both in those who "would not wait for the necessary preparation" and in those who were "laboring under other disorders."[8] Opponents claimed that the advantages of the practice were "imaginary" and that the surgeons "conceal'd or diminish'd the true number of deaths occasion'd by Inoculation."[9] The results must have been convincing enough to the public, for the surgeons and physicians were "suddenly oppressed by a great rush of business."[10]

In the spring of 1766, Jefferson's old classmate, George Gilmer, lately returned M.D. from the University of Edinburgh, sent a letter of introduction for Jefferson to John Morgan of Philadelphia.[11] Morgan and another Edinburgh graduate, William Shippen, were conducting inoculations in the city at that time. Despite the considerable risk and high mortality connected with the variolation technique, Jefferson underwent the process in May of that year with no ill effects.[12] In the fall of 1782, after the death of his wife, Jefferson took his children and his wards, the Carrs, to Amphill, the home of Colonel Archibald Cary, for inoculation. He personally acted as the chief nurse during their recovery.[13]

In 1799, another Philadelphia physician with Edinburgh credentials, Benjamin Waterhouse, received from London a copy of Dr. Edward Jenner's "Inquiry into the causes and Effects of the Varilae Vaccinae, or Cow-Pock," the substance of which he published in the *Columbian Sentinel* under the title "Something Curious in the Medical Line."[14] Dr. Jenner was able to derive from cowpox an effective vaccine for smallpox. Cowpox, first recognized in England, was found to be contracted by humans when milking an infected cow. Waterhouse described the disease as having "this strikingly singular property that it can be transferred from the Cow to the human kind, producing a mild distemper, never fatal, *and would secure the person so inoculated, ever after from the Small Pox.*"[15] Waterhouse was so convinced of the efficacy of this vaccine that he sent away for some of the virus and inoculated four of his own children and three other members of his family. To make certain that the cowpox vaccine worked, he sent his children to Dr. William Aspinwall to be exposed to smallpox. At the end of ten days, they all emerged without any signs of the infection.[16] Despite the successful outcome of his demonstrations, there were many who refused to accept the results and others who even believed that putting cowpox into children would have the effect of slowly turning them into animals.[17]

In September 1800, Waterhouse appealed to President John Adams

The Cowpock by James Gillray, 1802. Ganz Collection.
Courtesy of the Harvard Medical Library in the Francis A. Countway Library of Medicine.

for help in publicizing the new and safer procedure but received a lukewarm response. Next Waterhouse wrote a letter to Jefferson which included a copy of Jenner's paper.[18] Several weeks later Jefferson replied, "I had before attended to your publications on the subject in the newspapers, and took much interest in the experiments you were making. every friend of humanity must look with pleasure on this discovery, by which one evil is withdrawn from the conditions of man."[19]

Jefferson apprised Dr. Gantt of Washington of the advances taking place, and on July 17, 1801, the physician received samples from Waterhouse sent on "a thread … imbued with the vaccine virus."[20] When the first three trials failed to produce the expected effect, Jefferson requested that more samples be sent to Dr. Gantt and suggested transporting the virus in "a phial of the smallest size, well corked & immersed in a larger one filled with water & well corked."[21] This would protect the inner phial from the air, keep the vaccine at a more suitable temperature, and increase the likelihood that it would arrive intact.

At the same time, Jefferson arranged for a Dr. Wardlaw in Charlottesville to receive samples of the vaccine sent directly by Jenner to Dr. John Shore of Petersburg. Jenner had placed the virus between two plates of glass and covered them with lead. After arriving from London, Dr. Shore reported that the vaccine "proved to be perfectly active. It adheres to the glass like gum, warm water steam, or a little hot water is necessary to dilute it for use."[22] In August of 1801, Jefferson had Dr. Wardlaw insert the vaccine into six members of his own family.[23] On August 14, Jefferson observed that two of those inoculated showed signs of "inflammation & matter. some of them complain of pain under the armpit & yesterday was a little feverish."[24] The pustule took an oblong form with the inflammation about half an inch all around.

A week later Jefferson informed Waterhouse that Wardlaw had recently inoculated fifteen more subjects, "14 of whom very evidently have the infection, so that we have 20 now of my family on whom the disease has taken, besides some recent inoculations. some of them have slight fevers, headache, kernels under the arm, & one only, has a very sore arm. most however experience no inconvenience; and have nothing but the inoculated pustule, well defined moderately filled with matter, & hollow in the center."[25]

Waterhouse was ecstatic at the news and congratulated Jefferson on not only the success but on Wardlaw's use of fresh virus for the vaccine. He wrote that by Jefferson's influence the "practice of vaccination has been forwarded at least two years."[26] He encouraged Jefferson to give the vaccine to as many as possible as "a number of decidedly perfect cases in the neighborhood of Monticello, will give the genuine disease a currency through Virginia."[27] By the middle of September, Jefferson had inoculated "about 50. of my family and Mr Randolph & Mr Eppes about 60.

or 70. of theirs."[28] Through the efforts of Waterhouse and the influence of Jefferson, the practice became almost commonplace.[29]

Jefferson was so convinced of the benefit of vaccines to mankind that among his instructions to Meriwether Lewis was "Carry with you some matter of the kinepox; inform those of them with whom you may be, of it's efficacy as a preservative from the smallpox; & instruct & encourage them in the use of it. This may be especially done wherever you winter."[30] It was to be one of Jefferson's gifts to the Indians, a show of goodwill to encourage amicable relations.

Another dreaded disease of the time, yellow fever, was more mysterious and controversial in cause than the smallpox. The supposed source of the illness even became a wedge of political division and has been argued by some to have been one of the crucial issues in the formation of the American political party system. In the summer of 1793, conditions in the city of Philadelphia were pregnant with Suetonian presages: flocks of fleeing pigeons darkened the skies, comets streaked through the heavens, exponentially increasing numbers of cats were falling dead and putrefying in the streets, and most ominously "swarms of flies seemingly indigenous to the city had been driven off by a dense mass of moschetoes that hung over the city like a cloud."[31]

Philadelphia had not been seriously troubled by yellow fever for thirty years, but in early August of 1793, Dr. Benjamin Rush warned of a return of the disease, which the medical community called *typhus gravior*. At the end of the eighteenth century, Philadelphia was not only the largest and most cosmopolitan city in America, but was also its cultural, scientific, and political center. Earlier in that year a bitter feud had erupted between the Secretary of the Treasury, Alexander Hamilton, and the Secretary of State, Thomas Jefferson. The battle, at first, was over fiscal policy, but it became more vehement and personal with the news of the shocking events emanating from France. In the spring of that year, the execution of America's former benefactor, Louis XVI, had polarized the body politic into antagonistic factions. The Jeffersonians, or Democratic–Republicans, were Francophiles and favored the new democratic revolutionary government of France; the Hamiltonians, or Federalists, were pro-British and detested the French mob rule and anarchy.[32]

In early August, more than two thousand French fleeing the uprising in Haiti began arriving in Philadelphia, and soon thereafter an outbreak of yellow fever occurred. The cause of the infection took on political overtones and even split medical professionals along party lines. In general, the "importationist" Hamiltonians were confident the disease was being brought in from outside the region; Jeffersonian physicians were convinced the fever was local in origin.[33] The Federalists advocated a ban on ships bearing French refugees entering the port; Democratic-Republicans wanted to accept the new citizens. The Federalists, citing fears of importing an epidemic, demanded both a quarantine and a limitation on trade with the French islands; Republicans saw this as a disingenuous attempt to wreck their lucrative trade with the West Indies and to damage relations with the new government of France. While raising concerns about infection, the Federalists seemed more eager to score points against the French and the Republicans than to save Philadelphia from the contagion.[34]

To the inhabitants of Philadelphia, the threat from immigrants must have seemed all too real. By the end of August, as many as 325 Philadelphians had succumbed to the fever[35] and, on a single day in October, 119 were buried. Between August, when the fever began, and November, when it ended, almost five thousand citizens, or about 15 percent of the population, had perished, and another twenty thousand had fled from the city.

Jefferson described the symptoms of this plague as beginning "with a pain in the head, sickness in the stomach, with a slight rigor, fever, black vomitings and fæces, and death from the 2nd to the 8th day."[36] He related that it at first was confined to the docks and Water Street but had soon spread to other areas: "everybody, who can, is fleeing from the city, and the country people, being afraid to come to market, there is fear of a want of supplies."[37] He noted with scientific precision that "the fever which at that time had given alarm in Philadelphia, became afterwards far more destructive than had been apprehended, and continued much longer, from the uncommon drought and warmth of the autumn."[38] In the same letter without commenting on a cause, Jefferson observed "on the first day of the month ... began the first rains which had fallen in some months. They were copious, and from that moment the infection ceased, no new subject took it, and those infected either died or got well, so the disease terminated most suddenly."[39]

Following his own advice that no opinion is better than an incorrect one, Jefferson did not indulge himself in the political discussions and diagnoses of the disease until he had a chance to investigate it scientifically and observe it personally. He wrote to John Page that "on the question whether the yellow fever is infectious, or endemic, the medical faculty is divided into parties, and it certainly is not the office of the public functionaries to denounce either party."[40] At first he thought that the Federalists might be correct and that the disease was infectious and brought in by foreigners. His personal observations at Alexandria, however, led him to believe that "it is generated *near the water side, in close built cities, under warm climates.* According to the rules of philosophizing when one sufficient cause for an effect is known, it is not within the economy of nature to employ two. If local atmosphere suffices to produce the fever, miasmata from a human subject are not necessary and probably do not enter into the cause."[41] In other words, if the cause were local and environmental, it was not likely also imported and human.

It was not until 1901 that Walter Reed, a University of Virginia alumnus, discovered that the true culprit was the mosquito, *Aedes Aegypti*; but it is remarkable how close Jefferson's scientific observation and rationale came to the true answer. He demonstrated the salient points to the Comte de Volney: "it is originated here by a local atmosphere, which is never generated but in the lower, closer, and dirtier parts of our large cities, in the neighborhood of the water; and that, to catch the disease, you must enter the local atmosphere. ... Persons having taken the disease in the infected quarter, and going into the country, are nursed and buried by their friends, without an example of communicating it. ... These have died in the arms of their families without a single communication of the disease. It is certainly, therefore, an epidemic, not a contagious disease."[42] Jefferson concluded that these miasmata generally are prevalent in large cities in the southern part of the United States, typically in low-lying topography; that they occur in the months of July, August, or September; and that locals are less susceptible than outsiders to be infected.

Although it is doubtful Jefferson believed in the Sodom-and-Gomorrah injunctions that gathering in large cities was the cause of these infections, nevertheless, his claustrophobic bias against cities was reinforced by the spread of the disease. Jefferson wrote to Rush, "when great evils happen, I am in the habit of looking out for what good may arise from them as consolations to us: and Providence has in fact so established the order of things as that most evils are the means of producing some good. the yellow fever will discourage the growth of great cities in our nation; & I view great cities as pestilential to the morals, the health and the liberties of man."[43]

When Jefferson wrote to Volney about yellow fever, he considered the elements that provided a suitable environment for the endemic and how to control those elements. In doing so, he was both developing a new set of rules for urban design and setting the stage for the foundational designs of the academical village:

> but the yellow fever rigorously so, confined within narrow and well defined limits, and not communicable out of those limits. such a constitution of atmosphere being requisite to originate this disease as is generated only in low, close, and ill-cleansed parts of a town, I have supposed it practicable to prevent its generation by building our cities on a more open plan. take, for instance, the chequer board for a plan. Let the black squares only be building squares, and the white ones be left open, in turf and trees. every square of houses will be surrounded by four open squares, and every house will front an open square. the atmosphere of such a town would be like that of the country, insusceptible of the miasmata which produce yellow fever.[44]

Jefferson's observations led him to believe that infectious diseases were promoted by close proximity, unhealthy conditions, and lack of fresh circulating air. This clear link between public health and physical surroundings informed his vision for public architecture in the United States, as did his experiences in Paris between 1784 and 1789. Bombarded with novel concepts, fresh impressions, and exciting possibilities, he immersed himself in a myriad of scientific interests in the French capital, including public health.

Enlightenment Paris saw an increased concern for issues of public health by scientists and architects involved with urban renovation. In December 1785, the preeminent Paris Academy of Sciences, under the leadership of the Baron of Breteuil, appointed astronomer Jean-Sylvain Bailley to investigate the central hospital of Paris, the notorious Hôtel-Dieu. In their report, Bailley's committee confirmed the hospital's long-held reputation as a death trap. It was the oldest charity hospital in Paris, founded by the Archbishop Saint-Landry in 651 in the shadows of Nôtre Dame on the left bank of the Île de la Cité. A number of factors contributed to its fatal charm: it was situated in the most densely populated area of the city, with stagnant air, deficient and unclean water, little regard for safety, and a mass of three thousand patients lying four to six to a bed. Cross-contamination was rampant, hygiene was appalling, and one in four who entered the hospital did not leave—reputedly the highest death rate in Europe. It also posed a danger to other denizens of Paris as a polluter of the city's water, a fire hazard, and a source of contagion.[45] It is little wonder that Hôtel-Dieu was known as "the gateway to death," "antechamber to the mortuary," and "Hôtel-Mort."[46] Bailley's committee decided that "the hospital and its location, design, construction, and operation could no longer be left, as in the past, to accident, convention or expedience."[47]

As Paris was wrestling with this issue, Thomas Jefferson received a letter from Virginia's directors of public buildings requesting his assistance in designing both a new capitol for the Commonwealth and a new prison in Richmond.[48] The request came at the very time that concerns for public health, welfare, and psychological impact were becoming factors in enlightened architectural design.

Jefferson was convinced that conditions destructive to the body must also be debilitating to the mind and morals. To ameliorate suffering, hospitals must have fresh water, circulating air, sufficient space, sunlight, and appropriate living and sleeping arrangements. The same principles applied to prisons, where inmates suffered from a degeneration of the soul rather than the body. He was aware of Caesare Beccaria's influential work on prison reform, *Dei Delitti e delle Pene*, published in 1764. It called for

The Burning of Hôtel-Dieu in Paris by Hubert Robert, c. 1773.
Courtesy of the Sarah Campbell Blaffer Foundation, Houston.

punishments proportional to the crimes, segregation of the sexes and types of offenders, sanitary conditions, opportunities for rehabilitation, and solitary confinement in which prisoners would be safe from other inmates and could reflect on their crimes.[49]

To implement such reforms, it would be necessary to change the physical environment of the prison. Like other public buildings in colonial America, prisons were not much more than a large house, where all the inhabitants dwelled within the same walls. Form would need to follow function to accommodate the new methods and concepts.[50] The infamous Newgate Prison in London, rebuilt after the Great Fire of 1666, was typical of the old centers of confinement in Europe. Its clientele included felons, debtors, and smugglers, and prisoners of all types and of both sexes, who languished together in crowded wards. They were surrounded by filth and vermin and faced the constant threat of putrid or jail fever, a variant of typhus that often proved fatal. In 1750, this distemper spread from the jail to the courtroom to the adjoining sessions house, claiming the Lord Mayor, two judges, and an alderman, among others.

Five years later, when the Court of Common Council ordered construction of a new jail, George Dance the Elder submitted a revolutionary plan. Contrary to established practice, Dance's blueprints provided for three entirely separate sets of quadrangles: one devoted to debtors, the second to female felons, and the third to male felons. His plans also included large fireplaces, numerous basins, lavatories, fountains, and a chapel; within the felons' quarters there were wards for daytime occupancy and individual cells for nocturnal residence. Dance's design for Newgate also made a psychological statement. To the outside world, the whole structure appeared monolithic and windowless, giving the impression of hopelessness, despair, and impenetrability to anyone tempted to lead a life of crime.[51]

The utilitarian aspects of Dance's design and its psychological implications seem to have quickly spread to France. In 1785, Jefferson sent

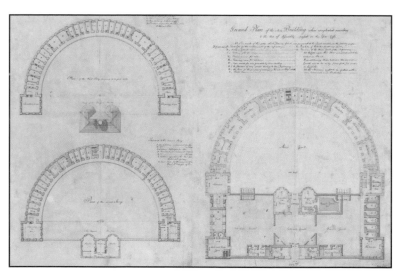

Jefferson's plans for prison at Richmond. Executed by Latrobe.
Reproduced by permission from the Library of Virginia.

Social Architecture and Public Health

the Virginia commissioners the plans for an innovative prison which he had obtained from its architect, Pierre-Gabriel Bugniet. Jefferson described it as "certainly the best plan I ever saw. it unites in the most perfect manner the objects of security and health, and has more advantage, valuable to us, of being capable of being adjusted to any number of prisoners, small or great and admitting an execution from time to time as may be convenient."[52]

The characteristics of a prison and of a hospital were strikingly similar in the late eighteenth century; in both cases, residents were confined in close quarters, with a lack of sanitary conditions which directly affected their health and well-being. Jefferson noted the utilitarian and scientific implications of the massive building programs under way in the Paris of his youth, in particular the plans to replace the ancient Hôtel-Dieu with four new structures.[53] For each of the hospitals, Bailley's committee called for a complex of separate pavilions where patients would be segregated by disease and given single beds.[54] Moreover, the new hospitals would combine patient care with medical teaching and science, paving the way for innovations in physics, chemistry, pathology, surgery, medical technology, sanitation, and hospital administration.[55]

In design, the hospitals of Paris were transitional edifices which incorporated a dimension for separating the inhabitants for more effective remediation and recovery, like a prison, and included spaces for observation and experimentation, like an academic institution. The design innovations Jefferson witnessed in the Parisian hospitals would reemerge years later in his plan for the University of Virginia.

In their search of models for the new facilities, members of Bailley's committee visited the naval hospital in Plymouth, England, which was described as consisting "of eleven large buildings and four lesser, the whole forming a square, but detached from each other, for the purpose of admitting a freer circulation of air, and also the classing the several disorders, in such a manner as may prevent the spread of contagion."[56] The committee also examined Louis XIV's chateau of Marly-le-Roi, which Jefferson himself visited on September 7, 1789. Upon comparison, the similarities between Jefferson's Academical Village and Marly-le-Roi, with its parallel rows of pavilions flanking a parterre, and the royal pavilion at the head of the terrace like the Rotunda, are immediately evident.[57]

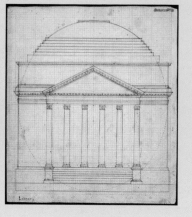

Jean-Baptiste Le Roy's plan showing
front view of the Hôtel-Dieu.
Courtesy of Johns Hopkins University Press.

Jefferson's Rotunda.
*Courtesy of the Albert and Shirley Small
Special Collections Library,
the University of Virginia Library.*

The plans that emerged from Bailley's committee incorporated features from both Plymouth and Marly. Two correspondents of the committee, who made suggestions for innovations in the pavilion plan, were friends of Jefferson: the Marquis de Condorcet and Pierre Samuel du Pont de Nemours.[58] Jefferson also read the committee's recommendations[59] for Hôtel-Dieu and noted that it "met a very general approbation."[60] On June 22, 1787, construction was ordered for the four new hospitals on the outskirts of Paris, each containing room for 1,200 patients. Each would comprise twelve pavilions built in parallel lines along a main axis and connected by covered walkways. At the head of the two lines of pavilions would be a chapel, and gardens were to be interspersed among these structures. The comparison between plans for these facilities and Jefferson's later design for the University of Virginia is striking.[61] Like the forward-looking Parisian hospitals, Jefferson's Lawn would afford good air circulation, a safe and tranquil setting, and reduced risk of fire and contagion.[62]

A lifelong champion of the "general diffusion of knowledge," Jefferson began envisioning the establishment of a great university as part of a larger scheme to improve education in his native state. At first he set his sights on elevating his alma mater, the College of William and Mary,

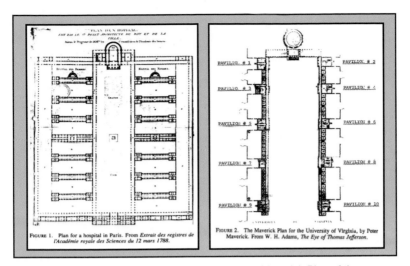

FIGURE 1. Plan for a hospital in Paris. From *Extrait des registres de l'Académie royale des Sciences du 12 mars 1788.*

FIGURE 2. The Maverick Plan for the University of Virginia, by Peter Maverick. From W. H. Adams, *The Eye of Thomas Jefferson.*

Jean-Baptiste Le Roy's plan for a hospital in Paris.
Courtesy of Johns Hopkins University Press.

The Maverick Plan of the University of Virginia.
Courtesy of the Albert and Shirley Small Special Collections Library, the University of Virginia Library.

but when the school's prospects looked unpromising, he began to devote his attention to founding a new institution.

In 1800, Jefferson wrote to the eminent scientist Joseph Priestley, a friend and colleague of William Small, about his plans: "We have in that state a college (Wm. & Mary) just well enough endowed to draw out a miserable existence to which its miserable constitution has doomed it. it is moreover eccentric in it's position, exposed to the bilious diseases as all the lower country is & therefore abandoned by the public care, as that part of the country itself is in a considerable degree by it's inhabitants. we wish to establish in the upper & Healthier & more centrally for the state an University."[63]

Jefferson's thinking about the ideal academic setting evolved over a number of years and was drawn from many sources, including what he had seen during his halcyon days in Paris and his observations of the disease-prone quarters of Philadelphia and Alexandria. In 1810, in a letter to the Trustees for the Lottery of East Tennessee College, Jefferson previewed his concept for the ideal academic institution. The physical layout would be predicated on order and space, not crowding and claustrophobic disarray–in his vision, constructing "one large and expensive" building for such purposes would be a mistake. Instead, "it is infinitely better to erect a small and separate lodge for each separate professorship, with only a hall below for his class, and two chambers above for himself; joining these lodges by barracks for a certain portion of the students, opening into a covered way to give dry communication between all schools."[64] The lodges and barracks, arranged around an open square of grass and trees, would minimize the dangers of fire and infection and would form "an academical village," a place that would offer "that quiet retirement so friendly to study" rather than "a large and common den of noise, of filth, and of fetid air."[65]

As in his plans for the prison at Richmond, this design would have the added advantage of allowing additional buildings to be erected as the institution grew and as "the funds become competent."[66] In 1816, in a letter to Virginia Governor Wilson Cary Nicholas, Jefferson suggested that the small buildings envisioned for what would become the University should be set on three sides of a piazza "to admit extension." He also expressed that the buildings should be "models of Architecture of the purest forms of antiquity, furnishing to the student examples of the precepts he will be taught in that art."[67]

Jefferson combined concepts from his extended study of prisons and hospitals to form a composite concept for his educational institution. Architectural historian Louis Greenbaum, in examining the link between the Paris hospitals and Jefferson's university, noted that the orderly arrangement of pavilions allowed for "superior fenestration and ventilation against 'mephitic exhalations and morbific miasma' and to isolate contagion and disease."[68] It also promoted natural interchange between students and faculty. In Newgate, the keeper lived in close proximity to the prisoners to be conspicuous and watchful. In the Academical Village, the professor lived in close proximity to students to encourage discussion, to engage in debate, and to be vigilant against youthful indiscretions. Benjamin Henry Latrobe, America's first professional architect, advised Jefferson to add a focal point to his ensemble. In the new hospitals of Paris, a chapel occupied this central space, as it had in Dance's design for Newgate. In Jefferson's university, an enlightened secular temple, the Rotunda, acted as the altar around which the other buildings stood in attendance.

Perhaps to no other single venture in his life did Jefferson devote so much of his undivided time and attention as to the establishment of the University of Virginia. The deliberate utilitarian purposes, scientific precision, and moral improvement inherent in his plans for the university elevate Jefferson from charges of being a gentleman dabbler with artistic pretensions into a presence that must be seen as "a modern-day architect and planner who anticipated the environmental, social and symbolic ramifications of a complex institution."[69]

5

Jefferson the Scientific Spymaster

My poor cipher! I meant to make it more complicated & increase the difficulties of deciphering. And Lo! I made it more unintelligible to my own correspondent.

—JOHN ADAMS TO WILLIAM VAN MURRAY,
NOVEMBER 2, 1799

Transmitting information in the eighteenth century was a notoriously dicey business. Correspondents of the day were constantly concerned that valuable or confidential information would fall into the hands of some scoundrel. Matthew Boulton warned William Small against sending explicit directions for perfecting the steam engine because "French spies are everywhere."[1] Virginia Governor Francis Fauquier flew into a rage when John Camm delivered a letter from the Privy Council that, being "open, dirty, and worn out at the Edges and Folds,"[2] had obviously been passed around to Camm's friends and Fauquier's foes. Whether for purposes of voyeuristic pleasure, commercial espionage, or political expediency, mail posted was not always received or delivered unmolested.

A young Thomas Jefferson even feared that his harmless and puerile letters to his friend John Page would be intercepted by nosy neighbors.

He wrote to Page in 1763, "if this letter was to fall in the hands of some of our gay acquaintance, your correspondent and his solemn notions would probably be the subjects of great mirth and raillery."[3] Jefferson also suspected that a letter to Page the following January "may have been opened, and the person who did it may have been further incited by curiosity, to ask you if you had received such a letter as they saw mentioned therein."[4]

To keep delicate information from becoming public, Jefferson resorted to various devices to thwart curious culprits. Assuming perhaps that learned gentlemen would not indulge in such base entertainments, Jefferson would use only partial letters of a person's name,[5] or a Latin form of the name,[6] or even an inverted form in Greek letters.[7] On at least one occasion, Jefferson went so far as to write an entire letter in Latin to his friend John Walker based on excruciating puns,[8] perhaps partly for entertainment and perhaps partly to confound local busybodies and little sisters. But his concern for privacy, even at such an early age and under such inconsequential circumstances, led him to suggest to Page an alternative system of writing: "I will send to you some of these days Shelton's Tachygraphical Alphabet, and directions."[9]

During the Revolutionary era, common ways of disguising messages included ciphers, book codes, and invisible ink. The predominant types of ciphers were variations of the transposition cipher, the substitution method, the homophonic cipher, and the nomenclator cipher. In the transposition cipher, the letters of the plaintext are simply shuffled, such as "etcrse" for "secret." In a substitution cipher, the letters of plaintext are replaced by other letters, numbers, or symbols, as in "xcbtcl" or "19 5 3 18 5 20" for "secret." In a homophonic cipher, the substitutes have several variations for the same letter: s = 3, 7, 21, 44, 82; e = 5, 14, 36, 89, 24; c = 91, 72, 62, 15, 8; r = 22, 71, 30, 9, 11; and t = 66, 85, 4, 19, 25. Thus "21, 89, 15, 30, 36, 25" would be read as "secret."

In a nomenclator cipher, words, numbers, and symbols are substituted for names, words, or syllables, as in 2 = Washington, 1694 = ei, 31 = fort, and 84 = brit. In the eighteenth century, the code sheets for nomenclator ciphers were regularly written on large folded sheets of paper. In addition, these codes could be expressed by either a monoalphabetic cipher, which was a single substitution alphabet, or with a polyalphabetic cipher, which included two or more substitution alphabets.[10]

In book codes, each correspondent would have the same edition of the same book. From a prearranged agreement, a certain code would indicate the page number, another might designate the appropriate column, and a third would point to the word to be used. The books employed were often those which were universally available and frequently dictionaries of one type or another.

Besides the conventional means of codes and ciphers, invisible ink increasingly became the answer to securing information. Usually part of the letter was written in conventional ink and the hidden text was inserted in "white ink" at the bottom to camouflage sensitive information. This device was also known as sympathetic ink and was employed by both the Americans and the British during the War for Independence.[11]

As relations with Great Britain grew more contentious, the consequences of sensitive correspondences being waylaid became more serious. During this period the use of codes, ciphers, and invisible inks became more ubiquitous and sophisticated. At first, American cryptography had the "informal shirtsleeve quality of a pioneer barn-raising,"[12] wrote David Kahn, but as the stakes increased, the hobby became a science.

Cryptology has venerable roots reaching back into ancient Egypt and China. In Machiavellian Florence, Lorenzo di Medici had Sandro Botticelli encode his famous painting *Primavera* with a diplomatic message. In 1628, Cardinal Richelieu employed a local mathematician, Antoine Rossignol, to decipher the encrypted communications of the Huguenots.[13] Rossignol became the king's official cryptographer and established a bureau for encoding and deciphering secret correspondence known as the Chambre Noir. Other European countries, recognizing the utility of such a department, established secret offices of their own. Two of the most renowned were in England, where it was called the Black Chamber, and in Austria, where it was known as the Geheime Kabinets-Kanzlei. In England, John Wallis played Rossignol's counterpart.[14] The British considered the enterprise so essential that during the War of Independence, the British Black Chamber had an estimated budget of £80,000 per annum.[15]

The Americans had no central clearing houses for either decoding or encoding secret dispatches and were, particularly at first, working in a very primitive environment. The first cryptographic incident, involving crucial information passed on to the British by a member of the Massachusetts legislature, occurred even before independence was declared.[16] Thomas Jefferson and Robert Patterson both proposed advanced cipher codes, but few correspondents had either the scientific aptitude or the patience necessary for such tedious work.

Between 1776 and 1789, "a larger variety of ciphers and nomenclators were employed by American statesmen and diplomats than in any other period prior to World War II," according to historian Ralph Weber.[17] By 1789, a regular code had been established for diplomatic usage, and by the turn of the century, the nomenclator cipher became the most common method of transmitting secret messages. Among the different ciphers and their variants used by Jefferson were the Dumas code, the Lovell cipher system, the Jay-Livingston code, the Dana cipher, the Lee cipher, the Patterson cipher, and the Monroe cipher.

The Dumas code was developed by a Swiss citizen residing in Holland, Charles William Fredric Dumas.[18] Dumas sympathized with the American cause and frequently collaborated with Benjamin Franklin. As Franklin's successor as minister to France, Thomas Jefferson knew and used this system, which was regarded as the cipher most reliable and available to the Continental Congress and its foreign agents.[19] The Dumas code required numbering letters and punctuation consecutively based on a specified passage in French. To keep the code secure, it was necessary to change the code passage frequently. For correspondents, this made use of the code doubly confounding, and the deciphering process was excessively tedious.

An alternative was developed by James Lovell, a Harvard-educated delegate to the Continental Congress who was appointed to the Committee for Foreign Affairs in 1777. He created a cipher that had both vertical and horizontal intercepts and a keyword and was comprised of a 27-item alphabet that included an ampersand. The x-axis margin would be alphabetic and the y-axis margin numeric, with scrambled letters running both vertically and horizontally. If the keyword was *Mary*, which both correspondents would know, then the coded message might read 27, 14, 8, 33. In column M, the 27th letter was S; in column A, the 14th letter was T; in column R, the 8th letter was A; and in column Y, the 33rd letter was Y. Thus the message would read "STAY." [20] Lovell's codes often confused his American agents, and the code words or letters were based on knowledge of a personal nature so trivial that the key was often unintelligible.[21] Edmund Randolph, in corresponding with James Madison, soon refused to use the Lovell code, which he found too costly in time and Madison too inept in enciphering. As late as 1784, Thomas Jefferson and William Short, using a variation of the Lovell code, also found the process too demanding. Jefferson failed to follow the sequencing of letters consistently, and thus Short frequently received garbled dispatches.[22] Even mighty Homer nods.

Francis Dana, the American Minister to Russia, developed a code which he used with John Adams and Robert Adams "which combined elements of the Lovell code along with multiple code elements, so that, for example, the code numbers for *Adams* were '28', '29' , '90'; and for *treaty* '221' , '252' and '283'. ...The Dana-Adams cipher combined the best elements of the eighteenth century American cipher, along with 80 names of persons, countries, and a few nouns such as war, credit, fishery, and mediation, all words which figured prominently in the negotiations of the times."[23]

John Jay developed a simple transposition cipher, which he used with his law partner, Robert Livingston, and other correspondents. For security reasons, the code differed with each correspondent, and it soon became impossible to use. In frustration, Jay wrote to Livingston, "My first letter was in our private cipher; this you had not received. My second, by the Marquis de la Fayette, in cipher, delivered to me by mistake by Mr. Thomson, and lost with Mr. Palfrey. My third, in the cipher sent by Colonel Franks, a duplicate of which was sent by Mr. Barkley. ...I had then discovered my mistake."[24] Livingston replied to Jay that he would no longer use the code because "you seem to be at loss about your cipher … and because it would be of little use."[25] Combined with the slow and irregular delivery of mail, the delay caused by a mistake in a cipher often rendered the information useless.

To avoid the confusion and frustration of the complex codes, William Lee, who was appointed a commercial agent to Nantes in 1777, recommended a simple transposition cipher in communications with his brothers Arthur and Richard Henry Lee, in order that the transposition was not too transparent, he suggested that & and *cl*, which had no meaning, be inserted occasionally to confuse others.[26]

The Patterson cipher was developed by mathematician Robert Patterson in 1801 and revised by Jefferson shortly thereafter. Patterson wrote to Jefferson that the "perfect cipher" should be equally adaptable to all languages, easily learned and retained in memory, written and read with "facility and dispatch," and "inscrutable" to all but the writer and recipient.[27] It consisted of substituting one letter or symbol for another from a table based on pre-established code words. Jefferson's modifications compounded the complexity of the original design, but in the end, even he was forced to abandon it.[28] Nevertheless, Jefferson was so impressed with Patterson's code that he wrote, "I have thoroughly considered your cypher, and find that it is much more convenient in practice than my cypher wheel, that I am proposing it to the secretary of state for use in his office."[29]

In 1801, Jefferson developed one of the most advanced ciphers for use in the negotiations with France concerning the Louisiana Purchase. It was a nomenclator cipher with 1,700 numeric elements that equated with whole words, syllables, and single letters. The primary recipient was initially Robert Livingston, the American minister to France at the time.[30] Jefferson was concerned not only that foreign agents might intercept and decipher messages, but also that domestic political foes might disclose confidential materials to Congress and the press. A slightly modified version, known as the "Monroe Code" or "Jefferson's Third Cypher,"[31] was introduced into diplomatic circles in 1803 by James Monroe, who had employed it in communications with Robert Livingston during negotiations regarding Louisiana and the Floridas. It became "the classic American diplomatic nomenclator," noted Ralph Weber, and was widely used by diplomats until shortly after the Civil War.[32]

In 1929, William A. Clark, a graduate of the University of Virginia, presented his alma mater with a treasure trove of historic documents, including a leather case containing a set of sixteen codes mounted on fifteen sheets.[33] As recounted by Julian Boyd, the late editor of the Jefferson Papers, the collection includes nine different codes consisting of a "series of words, syllables, and letters with numbers written opposite, and the de-

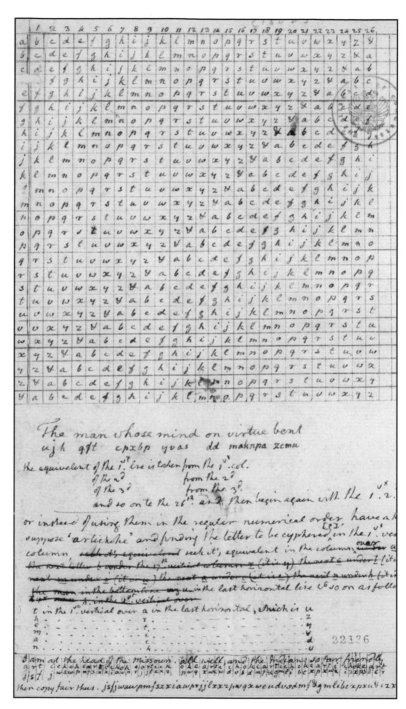

Jefferson-Patterson code.
Courtesy of the Library of Congress.

coding sheet being covered by numbers, ranging from 1 to 1,700 written opposite. Two of the codes are of a more involved nature, one being developed from a column arrangement of the Lord's Prayer which is likely a variant of the Patterson cipher.[34]

At least thirteen of the sixteen codes are in the hand of Thomas Jefferson. It is evident that they were developed with meticulous care and exhibit Jefferson's profound interest in the subject. Some of the codes are designated with the names of Jefferson's major correspondents and agents while he was minister in Paris. They are respectively notated Mr. Livingston's cypher, Mr. Pendleton's cipher, and Robert Patterson's cypher. Livingston's key was used between 1781 and 1783; James Monroe's key consisted of preset code words and was used between 1783 and 1787; Robert Patterson's key employed the vertical column cipher keyed to the Lord's Prayer and was used around 1802; and Edmund Randolph's key was a combination numeric and alphabetic key and has no dates connected with it.[35]

The advantages of ciphers included the necessity for security and transportability; the disadvantages were that most codes could be, in time, deciphered. Moreover, they were often confusing and obtuse, they were frequently lost or misplaced, they were time-consuming and tedious, and either the source or recipient often encoded or deciphered the message incorrectly.[36] John Adams was continually tortured by the ciphering process, and he was not alone. John Jay lost codes, mixed codes, and was stupefied by ciphers; Rufus King absentmindedly sent a message to James Monroe with both the code and the plaintext clearly visible, one atop the other.[37] Even such great scientific minds as Thomas Jefferson and Benjamin Franklin were occasionally flummoxed. In 1781, Franklin wrote to Francis Dana, "If you can find the key & decypher it, I shall be glad, having myself try'd in vain."[38]

In addition to the confusion, it often took months for communications to reach their recipients. Jefferson reported that letters had taken as long as "22 weeks and 4 days" to reach him. English packet ships were known for their speedy delivery, and Jefferson instructed William Short to use them for all but the most important dispatches. Benjamin Franklin wrote to Robert Livingston that "we are far from the seaports and not well informed, and often misinformed about the sailing of vessels. Frequently we are told they are to sail in a week or two, and often they lie in ports for months after, with our letters on board."[39] Franklin continued that, particularly in times of war, it may take "five or six months before the answer to a letter shall be received."[40]

Letters were so often lost that, in 1782, the Department of Foreign Affairs, under the directorship of Robert Livingston, sent multiple copies of the same dispatch by different transoceanic routes in the hopes that at least one would reach its recipient.[41] Loss was compounded by irregular sailing dates, destinations in the interior of countries, interruptions due to hostilities and embargoes, bad weather and sailing conditions and, of course, theft and carelessness.

One answer to the confusion of the various ciphers of the late eighteenth century was book or dictionary codes. In the book code system, multiple correspondents had the same edition of the same book and relayed messages by this means. The text, of necessity, had to be one that was readily available in case the original book was lost.[42] Although other texts were tried, due to flexibility and the alphabetic ease of looking up code words, the dictionary seemed to be the pragmatic answer. As a result, the most widely used spy codebook was John Entick's *New Spelling Dictionary*.

Entick's Dictionary was extensively used by both the Americans and the British. Francis Dana relied on it in correspondence with the continually confused John Adams,[43] and John Jay employed it widely until later switching to *French Dictionary* (13th edition, 1771).[44] In 1777, James Lovell endorsed Arthur Lee's proposal to the Committee of Secret Correspondence to use the *Entick's Dictionary* as a codebook,[45] and in 1779, Major Benjamin Tallmadge developed a code for George Washington based on the same book as well.[46] James Lovell informed Washington of the use of the same book by the British: "I found, as I had before supposed, that they sometimes use Entick's Dictionary marking the Page Column and Word as 115.1.4. Tis the Edition of 1777 London by Charles Dilly."[47]

Thomas Jefferson's and James Madison's favorite codebook was *The New Pocket Dictionary of the French and English Languages* published by Thomas Nugent in London in 1774.[48] Jefferson, however, insisted on such complicated guidelines for using the dictionary code that Madison soon decided to abandon it.[49]

Invisible ink was also effectively used during this period, and the gallo-tannic variety was well known to George Washington and his staff. John Jay's brother, Sir James Jay, a London physician sympathetic to the American cause, developed several chemical solutions for this purpose.[50] Whether Thomas Jefferson personally employed this means of conveyance is not yet known, but certainly his numerous communications with both Washington and John Jay make it a feasible supposition. Also the number of lacunae in Jefferson's letters indicates that his use of invisible ink is not improbable.

Jefferson always took great care with sensitive correspondence.[51] Because of constant confusion with complicated codes, the laborious transliterations of ciphers, and the frequent unavailability of chemical solutions for invisible inks, he determined that the most practical solution would be an invention that was scientifically oriented, universally utile, and a clear improvement in secret communication. Cryptology by its very nature appealed to Jefferson's secretive personality, and his experience as minister to France and his scientific contacts everywhere convinced him that Americans were far less sophisticated in this realm than their counterparts in the Black Chambers of Europe. Correspondence intercepted and revealed could cost many lives, change the outcome of battles, upset diplomatic advances, stop the flowing of foreign funds, and give one's political opponents great advantage. Jefferson's experience also taught him that the most brilliant of his friends and colleagues often found themselves befuddled when trying either to concoct or deconstruct a code. Jefferson, himself, and even Franklin, that most ingenious of men, sometimes were unable to untangle the Gordian knot of secrecy. Thus, out of personal interest and out of necessity, Jefferson's wheel cipher was born.

Silvio Bedini referred to the wheel cipher as being one of Jefferson's most important inventions, one that was entirely original with him, and one that could "have revolutionized diplomatic and military communications from the eighteenth century to modern times if Jefferson had applied it."[52] David Kahn, in *The Codebreakers*, described the wheel cipher as being "far and away the most advanced of its day."[53]

The invention was exceptionally brilliant in its conception and remarkably simple in its execution. Julian Boyd, the first editor of *The Pa-*

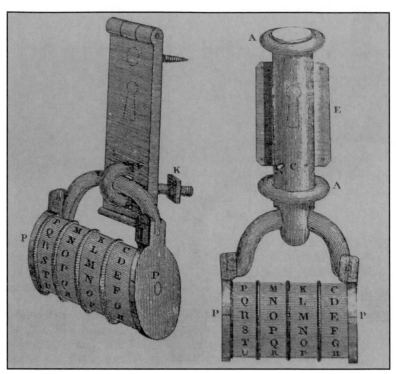

Edme Regnier's letter locks.

pers of Thomas Jefferson, conjectured that Jefferson probably started to work on the project in July 1790.[54] And Silvio Bedini cogently suggested that Jefferson's initial conception about the construction of the device emanated from the cipher locks used in the eighteenth century for safeguarding diplomatic dispatch boxes: "Such a lock consisted of four or more brass disks fitted interchangeably upon a central spindle, each disk inscribed along the circumference with a series of letters randomly selected. They were arranged in accordance with the keyword containing as many letters as there were disks, each letter of the keyword appearing on one of the disks. To open the lock, the letters of the keyword had to be aligned."[55]

The first of such Western cipher lock devices was suggested by Girolamo Cardano in the mid 1500s.[56] A combination lock that used letters rather than numbers was described in Diderot's *Encyclopédie Ancienne* in 1751[57] and illustrated in 1771 in a later edition of the same work.[58] The cipher lock reappears in the work of a Frenchman, Edme Regnier. In 1777,

Regnier won a first prize for his combination lock from the Société Libre d'Émulation de Paris. An illustration of the lock appeared in a scientific encyclopedia in 1785,[59] and a description of this lock appeared in volume VII *Arts et Métiers Mécaniques de L'Encyclopédie Méthodique.*[60] Jefferson owned copies of all of these books.[61] The transition from a cipher lock to a cipher wheel seems a logical and natural progression.

The cipher wheel was a brilliant adaptation and modification of this concept, but an alignment caused a message to be revealed rather than a lock to be opened. Rudolf Kippenhahn offered this simple explanation for its construction and applications:

It consisted of thirty-six wooden disks of equal size, each disk divided into twenty-six equal sectors. These carry the letters of the alphabet in random sequence. The sequence is the same for every disk, which presents no problem, since the number of possible arrangements is enormous. The disks are marked at their apexes with the numbers 1 to 36, drilled at their center, and mounted on a metal axis. ... Sender and receiver must possess the same collection of disks and must have them arranged on the axle in the same order. Let us assume that the sender wishes to transmit the secret message "attacktomorrowatsunrise." He therefore holds the axle with the mounted disks horizontally before him and turns them individually so that the letters standing next to one another in a row form this text. Then he locks the disks so they can no longer turn. If he now rotates this fixed block of disks on their axle, it shows another line. Every one of the other twenty-five lines is in an encoding of the message, in a form no unauthorized person can decode. Let us assume that the sender chooses the line that reads **TOBQMVES-BXUZKYGYMZAPXUW**. He sends this sequence of letters to the addressee, who then, on his own machine, adjusts the disks so that this same sequence of letters stands in a row. All he has to do now is look for the meaningful sequence of letters among the other twenty-five lines.[62]

Out of the twenty-six lines, twenty-five will be random letters with only one having a coherent meaning. Thus in an uncomplicated fashion, with little margin for error, even the most befuddled and absent-minded set of correspondents could securely send and receive important information.

Almost a century passed before another like device was invented. Around 1890 the chief of the cryptographic bureau of the French Ministry of Foreign Affairs, Étienne Bazeries, devised a cylindrical cryptograph comprising a central staff and two revolving and random polyalphabetic ciphers. It was remarkably similar to Jefferson's design.[63] At the beginning of World War I, an American, Captain Parker Hitt, based on Bazeries' work, reinvented the cipher wheel. The device was tested in Washington with ten secret messages, and after repeated attempts, their code remained unbroken. The American government began production of the U.S. Army's Cipher Device M-94 in 1922. Coincidentally, in that same year Jefferson's own instructions for making his wheel cipher came to light in the collections of the Library of Congress.[64] Like the communication concerning the Megalonyx, the instructions for creating the coding machine had lain dormant among Jefferson's papers for over a century. Scholars and military men were astounded that Jefferson had the skill and ingenuity to develop such a simple yet sophisticated machine more than a hundred years before the Army's trained cryptographers were able to invent a similar device.[65] Indeed, the foremost cryptanalyst of the time, Colonel William Friedman of the U.S. Army Signal Corps, is reported to have said he was astonished at Jefferson's "perspicacity."[66]

Bedini reported that the device was used by the U.S. Army until 1943, and David Kahn claimed that a version of it is used by the U.S. Navy to this day:

> [Jefferson's] cipher system, invented before the telegraph, was so far ahead of its time, and so much in the spirit of later inventions, that it deserves to be classed

with them. Indeed, it deserves the front rank among them, for this system was beyond doubt the most remarkable of all. So well conceived was it that today, more than a century and a half of rapid technological progress after its invention, it remains in active use.[67]

Kahn declared that, due to the longevity and the importance of this invention, Jefferson rightfully deserves the title "Father of American Cryptography."[68] Yet, even though Kahn and other eminent scholars agree that Jefferson was the inventor of this remarkable device,[69] questions remain. Some insist that there were similar instruments before Jefferson's time, but these devices seem to be letter-combination locks rather than ciphers. Deepening the mystery further is a device bought by the National Security Agency in 1983 and now housed in the National Cryptographic Museum in Ft. Meade, Maryland.

The former curator and founder of the museum, Earl Coates, purchased the cipher wheel from an antiques dealer, who in turn had purchased the device from a "picker" who had bought it at a yard sale. The story went that the original owner, an elderly lady, had found it as a child in the attic of her family home near Monticello. She recalled that it was

Cipher wheel.
Courtesy of the National Cryptologic Museum.

one of her favorite toys and that she had chipped some of the disks and broken several others.

The antiques dealer doubted such a device could predate the Civil War, and indeed, the museum also houses a similar apparatus that Union troops confiscated from Confederate forces in 1865. It was assumed that the device in question was also of that era. Therefore, the tale of the Monticello neighbor did not enhance the value of the object, which was being touted by the dealer as a tool of the notorious Confederate spy Belle Boyd.[70] But does this cipher wheel have a Jeffersonian connection?

According to a description by the National Security Agency's David Gaddy, a military historian who established the Center for Cryptologic History:

> Its size made it a "desk model," as opposed to handheld device. Accented letters showed its application to the French language. Its evident age and source made speculation of Jeffersonian association tantalizing and reopened curiosity about antecedents of the cylindercipher. The device obviously is incomplete: a brass frame, comprised of a base and two uprights, holds a wooden shaft on which are placed 35 wooded disks (probably boxwood) numbered in red ink–from spacing and numbering, evidently five are missing. The disks had been placed arbitrarily, some upside down with respect to others. ...Remains of a cloth covering– perhaps linen–can still be seen on the shaft, possibly placed there to keep the disks from slipping too freely while being adjusted. Other pieces are missing: evidently a horizontal brass bar held the two uprights against the shaft and perhaps served as an aid to viewing; the disks have 42 holes or perforations near the outer edge and were locked into place by a thin rood passing through an upright and through the aligned holes. On the edge of each disk, 42 characters (letters, including accented vowels; numerals, punctuation) are hand printed (not stamped or incised) in black ink.

(The accumulated grime and friction of handling and age blur or obliterate many of the inscriptions; some have been lost in the separation of chips of wood from the edge.) Each disk is numbered on the face in red ink (numbers 35, 36, and presumed 38, 39 and 40 are missing).[71]

Investigations in the early 1990s suggested that the device did indeed predate the Civil War and was likely to have been made in France in the early nineteenth century. Subsequent studies have dated the instrument much earlier, to the second half of the eighteenth century and possibly as early as the time of the American Revolution. Scholars also have revealed that the device is made of pear wood,[72] and while the letters on the cipher appear to be hand written, the red numbers on the inside of the disks appear to have been stamped. By inserting a thin dowel though a hole in each successive disk, a secret message could be arranged in a straight line. Clamps inserted on either end of the dowel would hold the message in place. If two cipher wheels were arranged in the exact same sequence, it would be an easy operation to pick out an alternative line of random letters and send it along to one's confederate. The recipient would line up the alternative line of garbled text, lock it in and turn the wheel until a coherent message appeared. If intercepted, the random line would reveal no message and the decoders might well attribute the defeat to a lack of their own ability rather than the true alternative. It was a simple but brilliant mechanism, which in its day would have been virtually indecipherable.

If the dating of the device is correct, and all current sources concur, several possibilities suggest themselves: The first is that it was developed before Jefferson's cipher wheel and had nothing whatsoever to do with Jefferson. Considering the agreement among distinguished scholars in the field and Jefferson's own statement to Robert Patterson referring to "my cypher wheel," this seems highly unlikely. A second option is that Jefferson saw Regnier's four-disk letter combination dispatch lock in Paris and adapted its shape and function into a forty-disk encryption device. The inclusion of French symbols on the wheel may have made the device more utile and adaptable to the purposes at hand. Julian Boyd thought

Jefferson probably developed the cipher wheel around 1790, which accords with this timeline.

In light of Jefferson's position as secretary of state, his concern about both the security of the diplomatic correspondence and the ability of American ministers to decipher or encode in an efficient and timely manner, and his hope of finding a practical solution to the cumbersome codes, this scenario does not seem beyond the realm of possibility. Several circumstances are very suggestive. Firstly, the device was found in a house near Monticello. After Jefferson's death, many of his items were sold to his kin and neighbors. Secondly, although the cipher wheel was, by all recent accounts, not reinvented until the 1890s, nevertheless, the cryptology museum's Confederate cipher wheel bears a remarkable resemblance to this device and Jefferson's instructions. Moreover, its original owner, a Captain Thomas Hawkins Clagett, Jr., of Leesburg, Virginia, came from a small town, again, not far from Monticello. And thirdly, Jefferson's own designs for the "cypher wheel" in his papers in the Library of Congress match the specifications of the Civil War instrument in many particulars. In other words, if one were to visualize the physical appearance of the cipher wheel from Jefferson's description, similarities with the model at Ft. Meade become apparent.

How did the Confederate Captain Clagett hit upon his cipher machine a quarter of a century before Major Étienne Bazeries announced his discovery in Marseilles in 1891,[73] unless he had seen a similar device before? And finally, is it pure coincidence that a device that so closely matches Jefferson's description of his invention and a Confederate copy of it both come from locations so near to Jefferson's home? The evidence to connect the dots is not complete, but what we know is intriguing and there is reason to speculate that the remarkable devices residing in Ft. Meade owe their origins to Jefferson's ingenuity and imagination. Perhaps the device itself, like Bru's drawings of the Megalonyx, was stashed away and forgotten by Jefferson, only to be found in an attic and treasured as a favorite toy by a shy mountain girl more than a century later.

Conclusion

When your mind shall be well improved with science, noth-
ing will be necessary to place you in the highest points of view
but to pursue the interests of your country, the interests of
your friends, and your own interests also with the purest in-
tegrity, the most chaste honour.
— THOMAS JEFFERSON TO PETER CARR,
JULY 19, 1785

Jefferson's devotion to science can be seen in his lifelong activities, his friends, his library, and his correspondence. As he declared to Pierre Samuel du Pont de Nemours in 1809, "Nature intended me for the tranquill pursuits of science, by rendering them my supreme delight."[1] The delights of science, although omnipresent, could not be compartmentalized to exclude the other sectors of his life. Therefore, Jefferson's pursuit of science became intertwined with the advancement of political, economic, social, and educational goals.

The promotion of an American agenda was the impetus and focus of many of Jefferson's greatest scientific ventures. While his efforts were regarded by some as extreme, by others as disingenuous, and by still others as hallucinatory, they led to some of his most productive scientific output, including his *Notes on the State of Virginia*, the shaping of the American Philosophical Society, the Lewis and Clark Expedition, and the establishment of an institution that embodied his intellectual and political aspirations: the University of Virginia. These and other ventures would lead to uniform methodology in scientific enquiry, codification of statutes and laws based on his scientific findings, and the foundation and expansion of new fields of study and the institutions that supported them.

Jefferson's Scientific Influences

Jefferson's first true in-troduction to science came from William Small. When Jefferson arrived in Williams-burg in 1760, Small was the only collegiate professor left standing in the battle be-tween the assertive Board of Visitors and the rebellious faculty. As such he directed not only Jefferson's entire ed-ucation, but that of his class-mates for two years, and his influence both on the direc-

William Small pencil sketch.
Courtesy of the Birmingham Assay Office.

tion of the curriculum and the methodology of teaching survived at the college many years after his departure. Both Jefferson and John Page at-tested to Small's influence on what would become a healthy obsession with science. Under "the illustrious Professor of Mathematics, Wm. Small," wrote Page, "experimental Philosophy, Mechanics, and, in short, every branch of Mathematics, particularly Algebra and Geometry, warmly engaged my attention, till they led me to Astronomy, to which after I had left College, till some time after I was married, I devoted my time."[2]

At Marischal College in Aberdeen, Scotland, Small was fortunate both in his teachers and in his mentor, John Gregory. Gregory was a cousin of Thomas Reid, the founder of the School of Common Sense

Marischal College, University of Aberdeen.
Courtesy of the University of St Andrews Library.

Philosophy, and co-founder with Reid of the Aberdeen Philosophical Society, also known as the Wise Club. Small transmitted the foundations of his scientific training and the underlying concepts of both the Wise Club and the School of Common Sense Philosophy to Jefferson intact and unadulterated. Thus the tenets of the Scottish Enlightenment—scientific method, utility, and improvement—became Jefferson's guiding principles, not only in matters of science, but in all of his activities in public life and as a private citizen. Writing to his grandson in 1808, Jefferson observed: "Under temptations & difficulties, I would ask myself what would Dr. Small, Mr. Wythe, [and] Peyton Randolph do in this situation? What course in it will insure me their approbation? I am certain that this mode of deciding on my conduct, tended more to its correctness than any reasoning powers I possessed."[3]

The second area of influence on Jefferson's scientific character was also a friend, associate, and correspondent of William Small, Benjamin Franklin. Franklin was preeminent in the world of science and dominant in the scientific capital of the New World, Philadelphia. Franklin was the sun in this universe around which not only members of the prestigious American Philosophical Society but most of the American intellectual community revolved. Many of this distinguished following were also friends and collaborators of Jefferson, among them Benjamin Rush, Charles Willson Peale, David Rittenhouse, Benjamin Barton Smith, Robert Patterson, and Caspar Wistar. These men were the scientific lead-

William Small inventory list.
Courtesy of the College Papers Collection, Special Collections Research Center,
Earl Gregg Swem Library, The College of William and Mary.

ers in America, and the American Philosophical Society became the premier institution for the advancement and promotion of the sciences in the New World.

Franklin and his coterie also established a widespread network of men of scientific interest and expertise abroad through the "Republic of Letters." The concept of an international scientific brotherhood that collaborates without regard to politics, religion, or nationality developed out of these cooperative efforts, with the underlying belief that it is a moral imperative to work for the betterment of mankind through the advancement of knowledge. Through such connections and his own efforts and abilities, Jefferson became familiar with an extraordinarily diverse range of "men of science" who both challenged and enlightened him. Among them was the great French naturalist the Comte de Buffon, who provoked and compelled Jefferson to conduct one of the most brilliant scientific surveys of his time, *Notes on the State of Virginia*, and to break new ground in paleontological, anthropological, and ethnographic studies, as well as comparative linguistics.

In this Republic of Letters, ideas were shared not only between individual experimenters but also collectively through those clearinghouses of knowledge—the philosophical societies or improvement clubs. Indeed, the same issues were often explored by the Aberdeen Philosophical Society, the *partie quarrae* in Williamsburg, the Birmingham Lunar Society, and the American Philosophical Society. Did this occur as the coincidental result of *zeitgeist* or purposefully through the agency of Franklin, Jefferson, and Small? Members of these societies operated in an open and selfless manner, free of concern about credit or reputation. This seems surreal in today's world of intellectual property that is jealously guarded and litigiously protected. It is interesting to note that Jefferson, perpetually in debt, never attempted to secure a patent or otherwise profit from an idea or invention that he thought might benefit his fellow countrymen.

Contributions and Collaborations

Jefferson's scientific adaptations and original contributions on behalf of his country extended to the mathematical as well as the mechanical arts. During colonial times and the period following the Revolution, each of the separate states had its own coinage and standards of measurement. Not only did interstate commerce often necessitate conversion of coinage and measurement between the states, but it was also required between the states and the estranged mother country. A coin commonly known as a pistole had a variety of values assigned to it, although according to the Reverend Devereux Jarrat, the rustic currency of barter could purchase "a good cow and a calf...and other things in like proportion."[4] The matter of uniform coinage was examined as early as 1776, when a committee composed of George Wythe, James Duane, Roger Sherman, and Thomas Jefferson attended to the matter. Their report called for a coinage expressed by decimal notations, as we have today.[5] The recommendation was deferred and not brought up again until April 1784, when Jefferson put together his observations in "Notes on the Establishment of a Money Unit, and of a Coinage for the United States."[6]

Without British controls, standards soon became so confusing, so inconvenient, and so open to abuse that establishment of both uniform measurements and a national currency became imperative. On January 15, 1790, Congress requested that Jefferson undertake the task of establishing uniform weights and measures. Jefferson made two alternative proposals: The first was a system based on scientific method derived from "mechanical operations, viz., a rod vibrating seconds…subdivided and multiplied…for every measure of length, surface, and capacity and these last filled with water to determine the weights and coins."[7] The second was based on a decimal system, using the old English names and making measures as close as possible to the old ones.[8] Both methods were confusing to members of Congress, and almost thirty years passed before uniform standards were enacted.

In 1790, as Secretary of State, Thomas Jefferson was charged by Congress with establishing a Patent Office and devising appropriate regulations for its operation. The first Patent Act was based on the British model, but Jefferson's bias against anything British, his dislike of the concept of restricting access to improvements, and the prerequisite that any plan worthy of a patent must be truly new and useful, made him a hard patent master. During his tenure as the first director of the Patent Office, only sixty-seven patents were issued.[9]

Among the scientific innovations that attracted Jefferson's closest attention were those potentially useful in the defense of the country: balloons, submarines, torpedoes, and steamboats.[10] On November 21, 1783, the first manned balloon flight took place in Paris, and Jefferson wit-

Montgolfier brothers' hot air balloon.
Expérience aérostatique faite Versailles le 19 sept. 1783.
Courtesy of the Library of Congress.

nessed the flight of the Roberts brothers in Paris the following year.[11] The manifold implications of this new method of conveyance immediately suggested themselves to Jefferson. Not only would the trip from Philadelphia to Monticello be shortened from ten days to five hours,[12] but also, as he wrote to Francis Hopkinson, in military warfare it could "threaten the prostration of fortified works...the destruction of fleets & what not."[13] Jefferson also considered the advantages of the balloon for military reconnaissance, transporting correspondence and materials through enemy territories, and distributing propaganda.

These innovations had implications for economic warfare as well, particularly against that "nation of shopkeepers," in terms of both depriving the British government of revenues and increasing competition from abroad. Jefferson wrote, "The French may now run over their laces, wines, &c to England duty free. ...inland countries may now become maritime states."[14] Despite Jefferson's foresight and enthusiasm, his promotion of things aeronautic generated more attention as a target of editorial wit than as a means for pragmatic scientific advancement.

Jefferson's exploitation of science for militaristic ends was not restricted to the air. On the water he investigated the potential of steamships, submarines, torpedoes, and a clever plan to extend the shelf lives of ships and to have them at the ready with a moment's notice. In 1813, he wrote to Robert Fulton, "in fact as we cannot meet the British with an equality of Physical force, we must supply it by other devices" and suggested that the other devices might include Fulton's plans for "subaqueous guns, torpedoes, or diving boats."[15]

The first American plan for a submarine had been transmitted to Jefferson by David Bushnell of Connecticut in 1787 while Jefferson was still in Paris. Bushnell described it as comprising "two upper tortoise shells of equal size joined together; the place at the entrance into the vessel being represented by the opening made by the swell of the shells, at the head of the animal."[16] Its restricted space allowed room for only one operator and it was able to submerge for thirty minutes without replenishing the air supply. It was propelled forward and backward by means of a screw rotor attached at the front of the vessel and laterally by a rudder at the rear.[17] The submarine also had a torpedo attached in the form of a powder keg. Bushnell had designed a place located "behind the submarine...above the rudder, for carrying a large powder magazine...within the magazine was an apparatus, constructed to run any proposed length of time, under twelve hours; when it run out its time, it unpinioned a strong lock resembling a gun lock, which gave fire to the powder."[18]

Although the torpedo had been tested under battle conditions several times, it was successful only once in 1777, and not even then with the desired result. Bushnell pulled aside an enemy frigate and released the powder keg, but "the machine fell in with a schooner at anchor, astern of the frigate, and [the frigate was] concealed from my sight. By some means or another, it was fired, and demolished the schooner and three men—and blew the only one left alive, overboard."[19]

With Jefferson's encouragement, Fulton attempted not only to make submarines and torpedoes practical but also to find new uses for Boulton and Watt's steam engines. In 1807, Jefferson wrote to Fulton, "I consider your Torpedoes as valuable means of the defense of harbours, & have no doubt that we should adopt them to a considerable degree."[20] But he cautioned him, "if indeed the mode of attaching them [torpedoes] to a cable of a ship be the only one, proposed modes of prevention cannot be difficult."[21] He suggested that a school for naval engineers be established to train marines in these capabilities. And ironically, as Alex Roland has written, "it was the great democrat and early foe of a military academy, who finally established a military engineering school at West Point modeled on the école polytechnique."[22]

In 1810, Jefferson convinced Congress to appropriate five thousand dollars for experiments with the torpedo as an engine of war.[23] Jefferson concurred with Fulton's assessment that a useable torpedo would render large navies extremely vulnerable. As late as 1813 he petitioned President Madison, with the endorsement of Stephen Decatur, to launch development of a submarine gun and promoted Fulton, a man of inexhaustible ingenuity, as the man for the job. Congress did not concur with these ambitious plans, but Jefferson never lost interest in advanced weapon design and application.

Jefferson knew that it would be difficult, if not impossible, to build and maintain a navy capable of standing up to the British and only hoped that circumstances would prevent the need for such a force until Revolutionary War debts could be paid and the national economy fortified. In public office, Jefferson was always looking for a more reasonable way of accomplishing an end. Congress was much divided on whether to build a navy and was much daunted by the cost of preparing and maintaining a fleet. In England, Jefferson noted, it is reckoned to be "cheaper to burn their fleet & build a new one" than to pay for constant maintenance.[24]

Jefferson recalled, "I learnt that, in Venice, there was then [during his Ministry in France] ships, lying on their original stocks ready for launching at any moment, which had been so for 80. years, and were still in a perfect state of preservation, and kept so by constant pumping."[25] Jefferson then hit upon the idea that the cost of the constant pumping could be alleviated by combining a lock system with a common wet dock with a constant source of running water in which the dock was above the high water mark. He imagined that Tyber Creek in the Washington basin would be the ideal spot for such an operation. He contrived with Benjamin Latrobe to build such a series of stalls that resembled the Halls du Blé in Paris, as well as "a construction of a lock system & dry dock over which a cover could be built so that the vessels could be preserved from the elements."[26] Again, Jefferson was roundly criticized in the press for what was seen as a wild-eyed scheme.[27]

Had Congress supported this plan, according to Jefferson, there would have been "a number of vessels always ready to be launched with nothing unfinished except the planting of masts," but Jefferson was unable to convince even those who favored a strong navy.[28] In spite of a multitude of failures and defeats, Jefferson never shied away from trying a new venture or novel idea. In his view, the shame was not in failing but in not attempting.

A Fascination with Innovation

One of Jefferson's greatest sources of pleasure was the modification, adaptation, and improvement of the inventions of others. In fact, Jefferson was so proficient in these endeavors that, in the area of science, he is remembered almost exclusively for the ingenuity of his gizmos. Among the more celebrated of his gadgets are the walking stick, a folding chair, a camp stool, an improved hemp-brake machine, a pedometer, an odometer, various clocks and watches, and a macaroni machine. Ironically, a fascination with the genius of his gadgets and gizmos has all but overshadowed and devalued his true scientific abilities and contributions.

Visitors to Monticello are most impressed with the Great Clock in the entrance hall, the polygraph, the double-acting doors in the parlor, the wine dumbwaiter in the dining room, the alcove beds, the triple-sash windows, and the all-weather passage that transverses the basement of the house.[29] Other innovative touches include the use of natural light through skylights and the use of dependencies to extend the space within the house.

According to Silvio Bedini, "Documentary evidence reveals that the Great Clock was designed by Jefferson himself to serve as a timepiece for the entire farm at Monticello and that it was installed in the entrance hall in the early months of 1793."[30] It was constructed with two dials, one visible from within the entrance hall, the other from outside the house. The clock struck a great bell, which was easily heard from both within the house and throughout the farm. Located above the main door, the clock was powered by a pendulum and a set of fourteen weights resembling cannonballs, each marked with a day of the week. Thus the device serves as both a clock and a daily calendar.[31] When the weights drop the full length of the wire, the clock is rewound. A miscalculation in construction necessitated that a hole be made in the floor, and the marking for Saturday resides with the winding mechanism in the basement of the mansion.

Also saluting visitors to the house is a wind vane on the ceiling. According to a Hessian officer who painted the design for the wind vane, "The Governor possesses a Noble Spirit of Building, he is now finishing an elegant building according to his own fancy. In his parlour he is creating on the Cieling a Compass of his own invention by wich he can Know the strength as well as the Direction of the Winds. I have promised to paint the Compass for it."[32]

Always interested in saving labor and perpetually overwhelmed with correspondence, Jefferson was understandably captivated by copying devices. The first device that he owned was a Watt copy press, which operated in a way similar to carbon copying but could record both incoming and outgoing mail. Watt invented the process around 1770; patent and production followed in around 1780.[33] Informed of the invention by

Benjamin Franklin, Jefferson ordered a copy press in 1783.[34] He purchased paper for the press from Woodmason's stationery shop while touring England with John Adams.[35] During their swing through the Midlands, Jefferson and Adams paid a visit to Birmingham, and it is likely that Jefferson first viewed Watt's copy press there.[36] In 1803, the polygraph came to Jefferson's attention, which, like Watt's machine, was able to make multiple copies of letters. The polygraph was developed by an Englishman named John Isaac Hawkins and manufactured by Jefferson's old friend Charles Willson Peale. An enthusiastic supporter of this invention, Jefferson owned twelve and gave them as presents to friends and dignitaries, but he was always looking for ways to make this device more portable and utile. This became the subject of an ongoing exchange between Jefferson and Peale.[37] The invention relied on parallel pens rather than cumbersome copy paper and was more easily operated. Later Jefferson experimented with a device called the Wedgwood Manifold Stylographic Writer, which used a type of carbon paper process, but it was messy and malodorous.

But the copy press was not the only scientific improvement from the Birmingham group which drew Jefferson's attention. Jefferson observed the steam engines, on which Small had collaborated with Watt, both in Birmingham at Boulton's renowned Soho Factory and at his new installation at the Albion Mills near Blackfriars Bridge in London.[38] The steam engine, originally designed to pump water out of coal mines, was being adapted to a myriad of applications, including one by Fulton for a steamboat both for the purposes of inland commerce and a "mosquito" fleet to harass the much larger British fleet in case of invasion. Jefferson promoted the use of these devices whose utility impacted him in a very direct way. He wrote to Charles Thomson, "I could write you volumes on the improvements which I find made here in the arts. One deserves particular notice, because it is simple, great, and likely to have extensive consequences. It is the application of steam as an agent for working grist mills. I have visited one lately made here. …I hear you are applying this same agent in America to navigate boats, I have little doubt but that it will be applied generally to machines, so as to supercede the use of water ponds, and of course to lay open all the streams for navigation."[39] While Small's former employer, Boulton, and his old collaborator, James Watt, were not present to guide Adams and Jefferson around Soho,[40] nevertheless, Boulton visited Jefferson in Paris in December of that year: "P.S. Since writing the preceding, I have had a conversation on the subject of steam mills with the famous Boulton, to whom those in London belong, and who is here at this time."[41]

In Paris, Jefferson's mind was abuzz with the innovations that he encountered. The wonderful novelty of the popular restaurant Café Mécanique at No. 121 Rue Nouveau-Palais-Royal must have delighted him beyond belief. The restaurant was constructed in a futuristic fashion that combined aesthetics with utility. Customers fortunate enough to secure a table were ushered in, the host would take their orders and transmit them to the kitchen below by means of a speaking horn, each table was supported by two hollow columns which connected with the kitchen from which the ordered meals emerged and into which the finished plates descended. "Tradition claims that it was Jefferson who introduced the dumb-waiter to the United States...he had a double dumbwaiter built into the two ends of the fireplace in the dining room [at Monticello]."[42] The Café Mécanique may have also been the inspiration for a device which still captivates visitors to Monticello with its cleverness, the lazy Susan. Plates are placed on the shelves, which are mounted onto the wall, then the shelves swivel into the next room—allowing both privacy from servants' ears and an economy of motion.

Jefferson also used his expertise to scientifically manipulate the flow of air and light throughout Monticello and did so by mathematical formulae: "light. Rule for the quality requisite for a room. Multiply the length, breath, & height together in feet & extract the square root of their product. this must be the sum of the areas of all the windows."[43] Jefferson was committed to making architectural specifications based on scientific principles and his dedication to this methodology is demonstrated by the way in which he directed the flow of natural light and fresh air throughout Monticello. In order to maximize the use of natural light he constructed triple height, or triple sash, windows, which could also be used as doors; instead of using solid wood for exterior doors he made partial use of glazed double doors;[44] and he installed thirteen skylights, including the oculus for the dome. "Equally important in this complex fenestration system were Jefferson's flexible provisions to control light, temperature and air movement."[45] To accomplish these goals Jefferson utilized louver shutters to modulate light and heat; Venetian porches served both as "cool retreats" from the heat and as extensions of interior spaces; and he even proposed the use of Venetian blinds between the columns of the west portico to keep the entrance hall and parlor rooms cooler.[46] For heating, Monticello had sixteen fireplaces which were connected to five chimneys. The chimneys were constructed in such a way as to force heat into the rooms à la Franklin and some of the fireplaces had firebacks that incorporated the design of the famous traitor, Benjamin Thomson.[47]

Father and Founder

Edmund Randolph wrote that "it constituted a part of Mr. Jefferson's pride to run before the times in which he lived,"[48] particularly in scientific matters. His enthusiastic embrace of areas of scientific advancement and utility left behind a wake of accolades and institutions. Because of his expertise and early promotion he is called by some the "Father of American Paleontology"[49] and due to his scientific approach to archaeology and introduction of the process of stratification, he is also known as the "Father of American Archaeology";[50] his devotion to the study of Native American societies and the comparative studies of their languages was a catalyst for American anthropology,[51] ethnology, and comparative linguistics.

FATHER AND FOUNDER
Father
AMERICAN VERTEBRATE PALEONTOLOGY
AMERICAN ARCHAEOLOGY
Founder or Originator
NATIONAL BUREAU OF STANDARDS
U.S. PATENT OFFICE
U.S. MILITARY ACADEMY AT WEST POINT
U.S. MINT
COASTAL AND GEODETIC SURVEY
U.S. DEPARTMENT OF AGRICULTURE
U.S. WEATHER BUREAU

His efforts to improve his homeland and the lot of his fellow countrymen led Jefferson down a path of unwanted political obligations and duties. Many of his scientific accomplishments in the political arena, however, were the genesis of later government institutions: the National Bureau of Standards, the U.S. Mint, the U.S. Military Academy at West Point, the Patent Office, the Coastal and Geodetic Survey, and the Department of Agriculture.

Convinced of the necessity of strategic defense mechanisms to counter a potential invasion by England, Jefferson considered a trained corps of engineers the most effective and probably the only realistic avenue of defense of the coast against superior British forces. In addition, French ambitions in the Floridas and Louisiana seemed ominous, and American ships in the Mediterranean were constantly being harassed. On February 16, 1801, Jefferson appointed Benjamin Franklin's grand nephew, Jonathan Williams, Inspector of the Fortifications at West Point, New York. On March 16, 1802, Congress authorized and Jefferson signed the Military Peace Establishment Act, which created the military academy and a corps of engineers at West Point. It also established a far-reaching precedent for federal expenditure in education, leading to the founding of many state colleges and the passage of the Morrill Land-Grant Act of 1862, which provided funding for technical and teaching institutions.[52]

On February 10, 1807, Congress authorized President Jefferson to initiate a survey of the coast to help ships navigate the nation's waters in times of both peace and war. The institution that Jefferson established to accomplish this mission became the oldest scientific bureau in the United States government.[53] Jefferson wanted the survey to ascertain the true location of coastal features, including dangerous shoals, by using astronomical positioning and mathematical triangulation.[54] Thus was born the Coastal and Geodetic Survey, which in time would give rise to the National Oceanic and Atmospheric Administration.

Jefferson's abiding interest in the science of agriculture impelled him to join agricultural societies in Charleston, Philadelphia, Paris, and London, as well as in Charlottesville.[55] As late as 1817, Jefferson drew up an agenda for the Albemarle County Agriculture Society called "Objects for the Attention and Enquiry of Agriculture," which concentrated on crop rotation, animal husbandry, soil conservation and improvement, and control of pests. The society grew as similar improvement clubs proliferated and began to cooperate and exchange publications. Encouraged by the success of the agricultural clubs and enthusiasm of others, Jefferson put forth a "Scheme for a System of Agricultural Societies" in which a centrally located society would serve as a clearing-house for agricultural information which would distill and distribute information and advice for mutual benefit. This proposal became the genesis for the United States Department of Agriculture.[56]

Greatest Scientific Legacies

It can be argued that the three products of Jefferson's scientific genius that best express his belief in scientific methodology, utility, and improvement are the *Notes on the State of Virginia*, the Lewis and Clark Expedition, and the University of Virginia. All three blended scientific, political, social, economic, and personal motivations and aspirations. Although John Adams wrote that Jefferson's "soul is honeycombed with ambition," it was not the ambition of wealth or power, but that of Cicero or of Cato for *auctoritas* and *gravitas*. It was an ambition that always sought an improved condition for his country, often by neglecting his own situation.

The desire to counter Buffon's assertions helped spur Jefferson to produce the *Notes on the State of Virginia* and was at the root of many of the objectives of the Lewis and Clark Expedition, but, as in almost every Jeffersonian project, the scientific was co-mingled and compelled by the more pragmatic considerations of politics, economics, and strategic interests. Some of the motivations underlying the Lewis and Clark Expedition were expressed by Jefferson twenty years earlier in a letter to George Rogers Clark: "I find that they have subscribed a very large sum of money in England for exploring the country from the Missisipi to California. They pretend it is only to promote knolege. I am afraid that they have

Lewis and Clark journal collage.
Courtesy of the American Philosophical Society.

thoughts of colonizing into that quarter."[57] It is likely that this was Jefferson's primary motivation as well. If the Lewis and Clark Expedition had the legitimacy of a quest for knowledge rather than a scouting expedition, all the better; if it obtained a vast store of new information in scientific areas, better still; if its conclusions resulted in a self-evident refutation of Buffon's theory of degeneracy, best of all. But other considerations delayed the venture.

In the summer of 1785 in Paris,[58] Jefferson encountered a young adventurer from Connecticut named John Ledyard, whom he described as "a man of genius, of some science, and of fearless courage and enterprise"[59] but "unfortunately...too much imagination."[60] Ledyard was the only American on Cook's famous voyage, and after his celebrated trip, Ledyard had attempted to raise capital for a fur trading business in the Pacific Northwest. Having failed in this venture and "being of a roaming disposition...and panting for some new enterprise,"[61] Jefferson suggested "to him the enterprise of exploring the Western part of our continent, by passing thro St. Petersburg to Kamshatka, and procuring a passage thence in some of the Russian vessels to Nootka Sound; whence he might make his way across the continent to America."[62] Ledyard did not complete his mission, "he had got within a few days of Kamschatka, when he was arrested by the order of the Empress of Russia, sent back and turned adrift in Poland."[63] Ledyard informed Jefferson that the Russians had established lucrative trading posts in Alaska. Financially, the Alaskan fur trade might be an enticement to American business interests, and geopolitically Alaska could provide a strategic flank for a projected invasion of Canada. Politically and militarily, knowledge of the great expanse of the West would be invaluable.

In January 1793, the American Philosophical Society commissioned the famous French botanist André Michaux to undertake a scientific expedition whose chief objects were "to find the shortest & most convenient route of communication between the US. & the Pacific ocean, within the temperate latitudes, & to learn such particulars as can be obtained of the country, through which it passes, it's productions, inhabitants & other interesting circumstances."[64] In a route that would have been the reverse of Ledyard's exploration, the trip was intended to start at Kaskaskia, at the juncture of the Mississippi and Kaskaskia rivers, head westward and north of Spanish territories, and proceed to Nootka Sound. The major stated objectives were scientific in nature:

> take notice of the country you pass through, it's general face, soil, rivers, mountains, it's productions animal, vegetable, & mineral so far as they may be new to us & may also be useful or very curious; the latitude of places or materials for calculating it by such simple methods as your situation may admit you to practice, the names numbers, & dwellings of the inhabitants, and such particularities as you can learn of their history, connection with each other, languages, manners, state of society & of the arts & commerce among them. Under the head of Animal history, that of the Mammoth is particularly recommended to your enquiries, as it is also to learn whether the Lama, or Paca of Peru is found in those parts of this continent, or how far North they come.[65]

In these particulars a number of scientific fields were addressed—geography, botany, zoology, mineralogy, anthropology, ethnology, comparative linguistics, and paleontology. However, Michaux's mission was also derailed, this time by the mistrust harbored by many Americans against the new Republic in France.

In 1803, Jefferson persuaded Congress to devote a nominal amount of money for an exploratory expedition of the West. In order not to arouse French and Spanish suspicions of expansionistic intentions, the venture needed to have all the outward appearances of a purely scientific venture. Jefferson's position not only as president of the United States but more appropriately as president of the American Philosophical Society gave increased credence to this stated purpose. If any foreign or domestic spies had watched from the sidelines, they would have seen highly technical and scientific preparations attending the trip. Jefferson enlisted the aid of the most distinguished men of science in America. He arranged for his chosen captain of the "Corps of Discovery," Meriwether Lewis, to be tutored in a variety of subjects by the most eminent men in their fields. For instruction in botany, zoology, and Indian history, Benjamin Barton

Smith; for instruction in the use of scientific instruments and astronomy and mathematics, which were essential for cartography, Robert Patterson; for instruction in surveying techniques, Andrew Ellicott; and for instruction in the latest medical techniques, Benjamin Rush.

Captain Lewis selected William Clark, the brother of George Rogers Clark, to whom Jefferson had suggested a similar expedition twenty years before. The instructions for Lewis and Clark read in many places precisely like those given to Michaux twenty years before. Again, the stated objective was to "explore the Missouri river, & such principal stream of it as by it's course and communication with the waters of the Pacific ocean."[66] Lewis was specifically advised the observations must "be taken with great pains & accuracy, to be entered distinctly & intelligibly for others, as well as yourself, to comprehend all the elements necessary, with the aid of the usual tables, to fix the latitude and longitude of the places at which they were taken."[67]

The specificity and nature of the explicit directions suggested that the objectives of the mission had more to do with diplomacy and politics than with scientific advancements. In regard to native tribes, Jefferson requested far more detailed information than he had asked of Michaux—information of a type that would facilitate relations with these tribes. The directives obliquely instructed Lewis to gather intelligence that could help determine which tribes would likely be friendly to the American government and hostile to other Indian tribes or the Spanish, French, or English. Jefferson also enjoined Lewis to "treat them in the most friendly & conciliatory manner," to encourage influential chiefs to visit Washington, and to allay whatever fears they may have of American intentions.

In regard to botany and zoology, Jefferson instructed Lewis to take note of "the soil & face of the country it's growth & vegetable productions" and to observe "the animals of the country generally, & especially those not known in the US." Paleontology would be served by close examination of "the remains & accounts of any [creature] which may be deemed rare or extinct." Jefferson was anxious to have as complete a picture of the climate as possible, and in the area of mineralogy, he wanted Lewis to find out all he could about "metals; limestone, pit-coal, & saltpetre; salines & mineral waters," as well as "volcanic appearances."[68]

The University of Virginia

Like Jefferson, the College of William and Mary possessed a strange dichotomy of nature, having, at one time, a traditional soul and a scientific spirit. After the Revolution, Jefferson wished to transform his old alma mater into a modern university, and to a certain degree he was able to institute extraordinary changes. Nevertheless, he envisioned a living, breathing institution that would adapt and change according to an educational *realpolitik*. Utilitarian advances would be made by teaching "all the branches of science useful to us," and they should be taught "in their highest degree."

The foundation of this educational plan was Bacon's *arbor scientiae*.[69] Jefferson advocated adding professorships of law, medicine, and modern languages to the curriculum of William and Mary.[70] Unable to institute the changes he thought necessary[71] and wishing to locate the institution of his imagination in a more salutary and central location, he began to cultivate support for a new university to be situated near his beloved Monticello. He wrote to the famous scientist Joseph Priestley, a charter member of the Birmingham Lunar Society, bemoaning the state of education in Virginia and outlining his incipient plans for a new institution.

We have in that state a college (Wm. & Mary) just well enough endowed to draw out the miserable existence to which a miserable constitution has doomed it. it is moreover eccentric in it's position, exposed to bilious diseases as all the lower country is, & therefore abandoned to public care, as that part of the country itself is in a considerable degree by it's inhabitants, we wish to establish in the upper & healthier country, & more centrally for the state an University on a plan so broad & liberal & modern, as to be worthy [of] patronising with the public support, and be a temptation to the youth of other states to come, and drink of the cup of knolege & fraternize with us.[72]

Jefferson's physical plan for the University followed utilitarian lines and scientific principles. It was designed for a logical and convenient flow of people and knowledge, form to follow function. It mirrored, to a great extent, the Paris architecture of Jean-Baptiste Le Roy. Le Roy blueprints for the Paris hospitals, noted Louis Greenbaum, "promised superior ventilation, economy, efficiency, cleanliness, privacy, and safety while cutting down on the risk of fire and contagion, and reducing noise."[73] Jefferson's plan for the "academical village" in many ways mirrored the concepts set down by Le Roy, both in physical arrangement and in health promotion.[74]

It was not only in terms of architecture that Jefferson intended the University to be a scientific institution but also in terms of curriculum and faculty. The first step, he wrote to Priestley "is to obtain a good plan; that is a judicious selection of the sciences, & a practicable grouping of some of them together, & ramifying of others, so as to adapt the professorships to our uses, & our means."[75] Among the subjects Jefferson enumerated to Priestley were "Botany. Chemistry. Zoology. Anatomy. Medecine. Natl. Philosophy. Agriculture. Mathematics. Astronomy. Geology. Geography. Politics. Commerce. History. Ethics. Law. Arts. Fine arts."[76]

He proposed that the "professors follow no other calling; so that their whole time be given to academic functions" and that the University should draw "from Europe the first characters in science, by considerable temptations" and by their projected efforts they would have prepared "fit successors & given reputation to the institution."[77]

Priestley opined that institutions of higher learning are intended for two classes, professionals and gentlemen who are "designed for the offices of civil and active life."[78] He advised Jefferson that for the professionals, especially for those in medicine, a greater number of professors are necessary, "as the business must be subdivided, in order to be taught to advantage."[79] For the gentlemen, Priestley thought it advisable to use fewer professors and give them only "the elements of the several branches of knowledge, to which they may afterwards give more particular attention, as they may have a disposition or convenience for it."[80]

Priestley strongly advocated a more modern composition of the curriculum, in which languages and divinity studies would be reduced and the areas of scientific orientation greatly enlarged and specialized. He concluded that professors should be engaged for the following areas: "1. for the antient languages. 2. The Belles Lettres, including universal grammar, Oratory, criticism, and bibliography. 3. Mathematics. 4. Natural history. 5. Experimental Philosophy. 6. Chemistry including the theory of Agriculture. 7. Anatomy and Medicine. 8. Geography, civil history, Law and general policy. 9. Metaphysics, morals, and theology."[81] Jefferson would eventually accept some of Priestley's initial recommendations and reject others. But like Priestley's general recommendations, there was in Jefferson's seminal conception a shift from the traditional to the modern, from theory to application, from the emphasis on elitist self-aggrandizement to utilitarian social involvement.

Science and mathematics were so ingrained in Jefferson's nature that they permeated every sector of his life. In his first extant letter he used mathematics in rationalizing his need to attend the College of William and Mary, writing "as I stay in the Mountains the Loss of one fourth of my Time is inevitable";[82] at the funeral of his childhood friend and brother-in-law, Dabney Carr, a time of intense grief, Jefferson calculated, by what he observed, how long it would take the gravediggers to dig up an acre of land;[83] and he planned a more extended education for his daughter than was usually requisite because "the chance that in marriage she will draw a blockhead I calculate at about fourteen to one, and of course the education of her family will probably rest on her own ideas and direction without assistance."[84]

Monticello and the University of Virginia are the two places most beloved by Jefferson and both reflect the importance of math and science in Jefferson's life. Monticello was so infused with mathematical equations from every perspective that even the size and number of windows were determined by mathematical computations; the rooms were filled with the dilettante delights of scientific instruction and entertainment; the very walls and furniture and conveniences were designed to delight and amuse and impress; every corner and crevice, every beam and tunnel, every convenience and piece of equipment, attested to his love of science and his genius. Monticello literally glowed with intellectual warmth.

The University of Virginia was scientifically arranged as well but in a more orderly, more clinical, more efficient, and more precise manner. The design commands respect and discipline. It expresses Jefferson's *auctoritas* and *gravitas*. It impresses rather than amuses. It instructs rather than entertains. It is a teacher rather than a host. Monticello is the archi-

The Rotunda.
Courtesy of the Albert and Shirley Small Special Collections Library,
the University of Virginia Library.

tectural embodiment of Jefferson's private persona; the University of Virginia is the manifestation of Jefferson's public persona. Together they reflect the strange dichotomy inherent in Jefferson's nature: in private, Jefferson was a patrician of the Roman Republic, the affectionate but austere Cato the Elder; in public, Jefferson was a child of the Enlightenment—Newton, Rousseau, and Priestley rolled into one.

Visitors to Monticello are often puzzled by Jefferson's desire to mark his gravestone with only three of his many achievements: as the author of the Declaration of American Independence, as the author of the Statute of Virginia for Religious Freedom, and as the father of the University of Virginia. His service as President of the United States, Governor of Virginia, and Secretary of State is left unmentioned. Perhaps it is because he wanted us to know who he was, not what he accomplished. He, perhaps, also wanted to express his often noted duality of spirit in the architecture and the purpose of his two favorite institutions—the University of Virginia and Monticello, tangible manifestations of his public and private souls.

Monticello.
Courtesy of the Monticello Foundation.

Acknowledgements

Several seminal texts are essential to the study of Jefferson's involvement in science: John C. Greene's *American Science in the Age of Jefferson* explicates Jefferson's role as the American promoter of the scientific ideal; Silvio Bedini's *Thomas Jefferson: Statesman of Science* speaks to Jefferson's lifetime involvement with scientific themes and their specific manifestations, while his *Jefferson and Science* provides informed essays concerning many of the individual fields of Jefferson's scientific interest; and I. Bernard Cohen's *Science and the Founding Fathers* interprets Jefferson's use of science in political, social, and religious contexts. All of these works have made great contributions toward both the understanding of Jefferson's impact on scientific advancements in the early Republic and his reputation as a scientist. I owe a great debt to these works, which were the starting points for my own investigations.

I wish to thank President John T. Casteen III and the Board of Visitors of the University of Virginia for both their financial support and their encouragement in this investigation of Jefferson's scientific contributions. I also wish to thank the President and Board of Trustees of the Earhart Foundation for providing funding for the extensive archival research conducted in Scotland and England, and Andrew O'Shaughnessy and Dan Jordan of the Robert Smith International Center for Jefferson Studies for the financial and academic resources they provided during the course of this research. A debt of gratitude is also owed to Maynard Garrison and Stephen Magee of the University of St Andrews for accommodations and privileges made available while conducting research in Scotland; to President Eugene Trani of Virginia Commonwealth University, who made my stay in Charlottesville possible; and to John McGinty, headmaster of Benedictine High School, who provided additional office space in Richmond.

I am grateful to my editors and advisors who provided clarity and focus: Bill Sublette, who with President Casteen was an initial supporter of this project and who moved it forward with a firm but calm hand; Peter Onuf, the preeminent Jefferson scholar, who kindly gave honest and accurate advice for both historical content and stylistics; and Keith Thomson, professor emeritus of natural history at the University of Oxford and research fellow at the American Philosophical Society and Academy of Natural Sciences of Philadelphia, who enlightened me concerning scientific aspects of this work.

Much of the research in this book derives from primary sources, and the result of many of the discoveries and synthesis of materials is the product of many hands. Among the numerous institutions and archivists to whom I owe thanks are Christian DuPont, Regina Rush, Ed Gaynor, Margaret Hrabe, and Heather Riser of Special Collections at the University of Virginia; Susan Riggs and the legendary Margaret Cook of Special Collections at the Swem Library of the College of William and Mary; Jack Robertson, Anna Berkes, Eric Johnson, Endrina Tay, Cinder Stanton, Andrew O'Shaughnessy, Leni Sorenson, Joan Hairfield, Jefferson Looney, Sue Perdue, Mary Scott-Fleming, and Bill Binswanger of the Jefferson Library at Kenwood; Elizabeth Chew, Susan Stein, and Chad Wollerton of Monticello; Gerry Gewalt of the Library of Congress; Keith Thomson, Charles Greifenstein, and Richard Shrake of the American Philosophical Society; Jennifer Wilcox, Jack Ingram, Jerry Coates, and David Gaddy of the National Cryptologic Museum; Barbara Oberg of the Papers of Thomas Jefferson, Princeton University; Francis Pollard of the Virginia Historical Society; Brent Tartar of the Library of Virginia; Rachel Hart, Robert Smart, and Norman Reid of the University of St Andrews

Archives, University of St Andrews; Fiona Tait of the Birmingham Public Library; Irene Ferguson of Special Collections at the University of Edinburgh; Ian Milne of the Edinburgh Royal College of Physicians; and Michelle Gait, Jane Pirie, and Alan Knox of Special Collections at the University of Aberdeen.

I also wish to give thanks to those who generously shared their expertise and experience with me: John Casteen, Harry Dickinson, Henry C. and Dixie Wolf, A. E. Dick Howard, Maynard Garrison, Thad Tate, Jenny Uglow, Sam Craver, Derek Alexander, Ed Ayers, Garry Wills, Doug Wilson, Col. Wray and Nina Page, Roger Emerson, Paul Wood, M. A. Sandy Stewart, Andrew Hook, Robert Arnott, Sir Nicholas Goodison, Stephen Gilmore, Spottswood Hunnicut Jones, Whitfield J. Bell, Merrill Peterson, Jennings Wagoner, Silvio Bedini, John Greene, Gillian and Robin Hull, and Andrew Doig. I want to express my appreciation to my research assistants Richard Graham Clagett, David Lowzinski, Eric Marquis, Whit Lee, and Adam Rodabaugh for their organizational skills and meticulous attention to detail, for their ability to catch my errors in annotation, and for their technological expertise which greatly enhanced the end results of the archival research.

And finally, to my friends and family, who sustained me and restrained me during this process: Michael and Debbie Binns; Dorothy Clagett; Arnold Pristernik; my son, Richard Graham Clagett II; my daughter, Alexandra Helena Bowen Clagett; and my long-suffering wife, Elizabeth Ann Clagett.

Appendices

1   Jefferson's Library

Jefferson amassed his Great Library between 1770, when his library at Shadwell was lost in a fire, to 1815, when he sold his collection to Congress. The topics covered by his holdings offer a fair indication of Jefferson's scientific pursuits. Between 1952 and 1959, Millicent Sowerby compiled a catalogue of Jefferson's Great Library, which can be compared with the Nicholas Trist catalogue of 1823. Below is a categorical delineation, by both Sowerby and Trist, of the library's contents. The categories of the Great Library and their contents were designated by Jefferson himself.

JEFFERSON'S GREAT LIBRARY

Millicent Sowerby [1]

SCIENTIFIC VOLUMES: 768 = 23.9%
Natural Philosophy [36]
Agriculture [80]
Chemistry [30]
Surgery [7]
Medicine [102]
Anatomy [11]
Zoology [48]
Botany [36]
Mineralogy [5]
Technical Arts and Education [24]

MATHEMATICS:
Arithmetic [37]
Geometry [17]
Physico-mathematics [37]
Astronomy [14]

GEOGRAPHY: (284)
Europe [66], Asia [30]
Africa [14], America [174]

HISTORY: 545 = 17%
Ancient [129]
Modern Foreign [181]
Modern British [113]
Modern American [97]
Ecclesiastical History [25]

ETHICS: 845 = 26%
Moral Philosophy [138]
Laws of Nature and Nations [47]

Nicholas Trist [2]

SCIENTIFIC VOLUMES: 899 = 26.5%
Natural Philosophy [35]
Agriculture [76]
Chemistry [30]
Surgery [7]
Medicine [101]
Anatomy [11]
Zoology [45]
Botany [34]
Mineralogy [5]
Technical Arts and Education [105]

MATHEMATICS:
Arithmetic [36]
Geometry [17]
Physico-mathematics [37]
Astronomy [35]

GEOGRAPHY: (291)
Europe, Asia, Africa, America

HISTORY: 521 = 15.5%
Ancient [129]
Modern Foreign [173]
Modern British [104]
Modern American [90]
Ecclesiastical History [25]

ETHICS: 837 = 27.5%
Moral Philosophy [139]
Laws of Nature and Nations [48]

Religion [190]
Equity [43]
Common Law [305]
Law Merchant [10]
Law Maritime [17]
Law Ecclesiastic [19]
Foreign Law [76]

Moral Philosophy
[POLITICS]: 374 = 11.5%

ARTS: 391 = 12.2%
Architecture [43]
Gardening, Painting, Sculpture [25]
Music [10]
Epic Poetry [43]
Tales and Fables [70]
Pastorals [68]
Didactic [69]
Tragedy [33]
Comedy [30]

FINE ARTS: 294 = 9%
Dialogue, Epistolary [29]
Logic, Rhetoric,
   Orations [23]
Criticism–Theory [18]
Criticism–Bibliography [25]
Criticism–Language [155]
Polygraphical [44]

TOTAL: 3203

Religion [188]
Equity [41]
Common Law [300]
Law Merchant [10]
Law Maritime [16]
Law Ecclesiastic [19]
Foreign Law [76]

Moral Philosophy
[POLITICS]: 451 = 13.5%

ARTS: 369 = 11%
Architecture [30]
Gardening, Painting, Sculpture [24]
Music [9]
Epic Poetry [41]
Tales and Fables [71]
Pastorals [66]
Didactic [66]
Tragedy [33]
Comedy [29]

FINE ARTS: 301 = 9%
Dialogue, Epistolary [28]
Logic, Rhetoric, Orations [39]

Criticism–Theory [14]
Criticism–Bibliography [23]
Criticism–Language [155]
Polygraphical [42]

TOTAL: 3378

---

2 Scientific Correspondents: Selected List

John Adams
Jean-Sylvain Bailley
Benjamin Smith Barton
Benjamin Benneker
Matthew Boulton
Comte de Buffon
David Bushnell
Marquis de Chastellux

Jose Correa de Serra
Pierre-Samuel du Pont de Nemours
Andrew Ellicott
Benjamin Franklin
Robert Fulton
Baron Frederic von Grimm
Benjamin Hawkins
Baron Alexander von Humboldt

David Humphreys
Edward Jenner
Jean-Baptiste Le Roy
John Ledyard
Robert Livingston
Reverend James Madison
Philip Mazzei
André Michaux
James Monroe
Louis Guilaume Otto
John Page
Robert Patterson
Charles Willson Peale
Joseph Priestley

Constantine Rafinesque
David Rittenhouse
Benjamin Rush
Sir John Sinclair
William Small
Ezra Stiles
Charles Thomson
Comte de Volney
Benjamin Waterhouse
Eli Whitney
James Wilkinson
Lewis Wiss
Caspar Wistar
John Witherspoon

3   Scientific Equipment: Partial Inventory

From items listed in Jefferson's *Memorandum Books*

Astronomical clocks
Barometers
Camera Obscura
Circumferentor
Compasses
Concave mirror
Dials
Dynameter
Electrical Machine
Electrophorus
Glass Machine
Globes
Graph meter
Hoisting machine
Hydralic engine
Hydrometers
Hydrostatic balance
Hygrometers
Lenses
Levels
Lightning rods
Magnifiers
Metronome
Microscopes
Magnetic needle

Odometers
Optique
Pantograph
Pedometers
Perspective glass
Perspective machine
Phials
Polycrest machine
Polygraphs
Protractors
Pumps
Quadrants
Reflecting Circles
Rulers
Sand glasses
Scales
Scioptric ball
Sextants
Steelyards
Surveying chains
Telescopes
Theodolites
Thermometers
Weather glasses
Wind vane

4 Scientific Honors

1780	Elected Member of American Philosophical Society
1783	Honorary Degree: the College of William and Mary
1785	Elected Member of the South Carolina Society for the Promotion and Improvement of Agriculture
1786	Honorary Degree: Yale University
1787	Honorary Degree: Harvard University
1790	Elected Member of American Academy of Arts and Sciences
1797	Elected President of the American Philosophical Society
	Elected Member of London Board of Agriculture
	Elected Member of the Linnaean Society of Philadelphia
	Elected Member of the Linnaean Society of Paris
1809	Elected Member of the Dutch Institute of Sciences, of Literature and of Fine Arts
1813	Elected Member of Antiquarian Society of Charleston
	Elected Member of American Antiquarian Society
1814	Elected Member of Academy of Sciences and Agronomic Society of Bavaria

5 Scientific Publications

1781	Notes on the State of Virginia
1784	Notes on the Establishment of a Money Unit
1786	Statistical Account of the United States
	Encyclopedie Methodique
1788	Observations on the Whale Fisheries
1790	Report on Copper Coinage
1790	Final State of the Report on Weights and Measures
1791	Report of the Secretary of State on the Petition of Joseph Isaaks, of Newport, in Rhode Island
1792	Circular on the Hessian Fly
1799	The Description of the Mould-Board of the least Resistence and of the most easiest and most Certain Construction
1799	A Memoir on the Discovery of certain Bones of a Quadruped of the Clawed Kind in the Western Parts of Virginia
1799	General Principles and Construction of a Submarine Vessel communicated by D Bushnell of Connecticut, the Inventor, in a letter of October 1787, to Thomas Jefferson
1799	Experiments upon Magnetism communicated in a Letter to Thomas Jefferson, President of the American Philosophical Society, by the Reverend James Madison, President of the College of William and Mary
1806	Message from the President of the United States, Communicating Discoveries Made in Exploring the Missouri, the Red River, and the Wabash, by Captains Lewis and Clark, Doctor Sibley and Mr. Dunbar, with a Statistical Account of the Counties Adjacent

Bibliography

Primary Sources: Manuscripts

Annan, Robert to Bird Wilson. 16 May 1805. Montgomery Collection. Pennsylvania Historical Society.

Boulton-Watt Collection. Archives, Birmingham Public Library. Birmingham, England.

Faculty and Alumni of the College of William and Mary. Special Collections. College of William and Mary. Williamsburg, Virginia.

Jarratt, Devereux. *The Life of the Reverend Devereux Jarratt.* (Baltimore: Warner and Hanna, 1806)

Jefferson, Thomas to Caspar Wistar. 3 February 1803. Cl.1987.32.A.B. (LFP/Box 82/ Folder 07) Archives. Clermont State Historical Site. Germantown, New York.

Jefferson, Thomas. *The Thomas Jefferson Papers.* Library of Congress. Washington, D.C.

Journal of the Meetings of the Governors and Board of Visitors of the College of William and Mary. Fulham MSS. Library of Congress, Washington, D.C.

Lewis, Warner to Walter Jones. 8 July 1766. Edrington Collection. MSS 1 Ed 745a 437. Virginia Historical Society. Richmond, Virginia.

Manuscript: Comparative Vocabulary of Several Indian Languages. Class 497. No. J35. Library. American Philosophical Society. Philadelphia, Pennsylvania.

Notes Prepared by Julian Boyd. Item 35054. Albert and Shirley Small Collection. Harrison Institute. University of Virginia. Charlottesville, Virginia.

Thomas Jefferson Cipher Codes Used for Diplomatic Correspondence. Accession #38-285. TB 56. Albert and Shirley Small Collection. Harrison Institute. University of Virginia. Charlottesville, Virginia.

Wright, James to John Bartram. Archives. British Museum. London, England. MSS. 21648. (333-334)

Primary Sources: Printed

Abercromby, James. *The Letter Books of James Abercromby, Colonial Agent, 1751–1773*. [eds.] John Van Horne and George Reese (Richmond: Virginia State Library, 1991)

Dinwiddie, Robert. *The Official Records of Robert Dinwiddie*. [ed.] R. A. Brock (Richmond: Virginia Historical Society, 1883)

Fauquier, Francis. *The Official Papers of Francis Fauquier*. [ed.] George Reese. (Charlottesville: University Press of Virginia, 1981)

Franklin, Benjamin. *The Papers of Benjamin Franklin*. [ed.] William Wilcox (New Haven: Yale University Press, 1983)

Franklin, Benjamin and William Heberden. *Some Account of the Success of Inoculation for the Small-Pox in England and America*. (London: William Strahan, 1759)

Jefferson, Thomas. *The Complete Jefferson*. [ed.] Saul Padover. (New York: Tudor Publishing Company, 1943)

———. *Jefferson's Memorandum Books*. [eds.] James Bear and Lucia Stanton (Princeton: Princeton University Press, 1997)

———. *Life and Select Writings*. [eds.] Adrianne Koch and William Peden (New York, 1944).

———. *Notes on the State of Virginia*. 917.55 J35. American Philosophical Society (Jefferson's Presentation Copy, 1782)

———. *Notes on the State of Virginia*. [ed.] William Peden. (Chapel Hill: University of North Carolina Press, 1995)

———. *The Papers of Thomas Jefferson*. [ed.] Julian Boyd et al. (Princeton: Princeton University Press)

———. *The Papers of Thomas Jefferson: Retirement Series*. [ed.] Jefferson Looney (Princeton: Princeton University Press, 2004)

———. *The Quotable Jefferson*. [ed.] John Kaminski (Princeton: Princeton University Press, 2006)

———. *Thomas Jefferson: Writings*. [ed.] Merrill Peterson (New York: Viking Press, 1984)

———. *Thomas Jefferson's Garden Book: 1766–1824*. [ed.] E. Morris Betts (Charlottesville: Thomas Jefferson Memorial Foundation, 1999)

———. *Thomas Jefferson's Library: A Catalog with the Entries in His Own Hand*. [eds.] James Gilreath and Doug Wilson (Washington, D.C.: Library of Congress, 1989)

———. *The Writings of Thomas Jefferson*. [eds.] Albert Bergh and Andrew Lipscomb (Washington, D.C.: The Thomas Jefferson Memorial Foundation, 1903)

———. *The Writings of Thomas Jefferson*. [ed.] Paul L. Ford (New York: G.P. Putnam's Sons, 1897)

———. *Writings of Thomas Jefferson*. [ed.] H. A. Washington (Washington, D.C.: Taylor & Maury, 1853)

Madison, James. *The Papers of James Madison: Presidential Series*. [ed.] J. C. A. Stagg. (Charlottesville: University Press of Virginia, 1992)

The Revolutionary Diplomatic Correspondence of the United States. Vol. IV (Washington, D.C.: Government Printing Office, 1889)

Tucker, George. *Letters from Virginia*. (Baltimore: J. Robinson, 1816)

Washington, George. *The Writings of George Washington from Original Manuscript Sources, 1745–1799*. [ed.] John Fitzpatrick. Vol. XV (Washington, D.C.: Government Printing Office, 1938)

Wilson, James. *The Works of James Wilson*. [ed.] James McKloskey.

Secondary Sources: Books

Adams, W. H. [ed.] *The Eye of Thomas Jefferson.* (Washington, D.C.: National Gallery of Art, 1976)

Bedini, Silvio. *Thomas Jefferson and American Vertebrate Paleontology.* (Charlottesville: Commonwealth of Virginia, 1985)

———. *Thomas Jefferson: Statesman of Science.* (New York: Macmillan and Company, 1990)

———. *Thomas Jefferson and His Copying Machines.* (Charlottesville: University Press of Virginia, 1984)

Bieder, Robert. *Science Encounters the Indian, 1820–1880.* (Norman: University of Oklahoma Press, 1986)

Bruce, William C. *Benjamin Franklin: Self Revealed.* Vol. II (New York: G. P. Putnam's Sons, 1917)

Carter, Jennifer and Colin McLaren. *Crown and Gown.* (Aberdeen: Aberdeen University Press, 1995)

Catesby, Mark. *The Natural History of Carolina, Florida and the Bahama Islands.* Vol. II (London, 1743)

Ceram, C. W. *The First American: A Story of North American Archaeology.* (New York: Harcourt Brace Jovanovich, 1972)

Cohen, I. Bernard. *Science and the Founding Fathers.* (New York: W.W. Norton and Company, 1995)

Commanger, H. S. *Jefferson, Nationalism, and the Enlightenment.* (New York: George Braziller, 1986)

Daumas, Maurice. *Scientific Instruments of the Seventeenth and Eighteenth Centuries.* (New York: Praeger Publishers, 1972)

Diamond, Peter. *Common Sense and Improvement.* (Berlin: Die Deutsche Biblothek, 1998)

French, Allen. *General Gage's Informers.* (Ann Arbor: University of Michigan Press, 1932)

Friedman, William. *Six Lectures on Cryptology: The Friedman Legacy.* (Ft. Meade: National Security Agency, 1992)

Gray, Edward. *New World Babel.* (Princeton: Princeton University Press, 1999)

Gray, James. *History of the Royal Medical Society: 1737–1937.* [ed.] Douglas Guthrie (Edinburgh: University Press, 1952)

Hankins, Thomas. *Science and the Enlightenment.* (Cambridge: Cambridge University Press, 1985)

Halsey, Robert. *How the President, Thomas Jefferson, and Doctor Benjamin Waterhouse Established Vaccination as a Public Health Procedure.* (New York: New York Academy of Medicine, 1936)

Hindle, Brooke. *The Pursuit of Science in Revolutionary America: 1735–1789.* (Chapel Hill: University of North Carolina Press, 1956)

The Jefferson Papers: Part II. [ed.] John Casteen and Anne Freudenberg (Charlottesville: University Press of Virginia, 1973)

Kahn, David. *The Codebreakers.* (New York: Scribner, 1996)

Kippenhahn, Rudolf. *Code Breaking: A History and Exploration.* (New York: Overlook Press, 1999)

Landsman, Ned. *From Colonials to Provincials: American Thought and Culture, 1680–1760.* (New York: Twayne Publishers, 1985)

Martin, Edwin. *Thomas Jefferson: Scientist.* (New York: Henry Schuman, 1952)

Meyer, Donald H. *The Democratic Enlightenment*. (New York: G.P. Putnam's Sons, 1976)

Mitchell, Samuel. *A Discourse on the Character and Services of Thomas Jefferson*. (Charlottesville: University of Virginia, 1982)

Morpurgo, J.E. *Their Majesties' Royall Colledge: the College of William and Mary in the Seventeenth and Eighteenth Centuries*. (Washington, D.C.: Hennage Creative Printers, 1976).

Morton, Richard. *Colonial Virginia*. (Chapel Hill: University of North Carolina Press, 1960)

Neiman, Fraser. *The Henley-Horrocks Inventory*. (Williamsburg: Botetourt Biographical Society, 1968)

Newton, David. *Encyclopedia of Cryptology*. (Denver: ABD-CLIO Publishers, 1997)

Newton, Isaac. *Philosophical Writings*. [ed.] Andrew Janiak (Cambridge: Cambridge University Press, 2004)

O'Neal, W. B. *Jefferson's Buildings at the University of Virginia: The Rotunda*. (Charlottesville: University of Virginia Press, 1960)

Onuf, Peter. *Jefferson's Empire*. (Charlottesville: University Press of Virginia, 2000)

Peterson, Merrill. *Thomas Jefferson and the New Nation: A Biography*. (Oxford: Oxford University Press, 1970)

Philosophy and Science in the Scottish Enlightenment. [ed.] Peter Jones (Edinburgh: John Donal Publishers, 1988)

Schofield, Robert. *A Scientific Autobiography of Joseph Priestley*. (1733–1804). (Cambridge: M.I.T. Press, 1966)

Sheehan, Bernard. *Seeds of Extinction*. (Chapel Hill: University of North Carolina Press, 1973)

Uglow, Jenny. *The Lunar Men*. (New York: Farrar, Straus and Giroux, 2002)

Vater, Johann. *Mithridates*. (Berlin: Vossischen Buchhandlung, 1812)

A Virginia Farmer. *Farm Management: The Treatises of Cato and Varro; Done into English*. (New York: Macmillan and Company, 1913)

Wallace, Anthony F. C. *Jefferson and the Indians*. (Cambridge: Harvard University Press, 1999)

Weber, Ralph. *Marked Dispatches: Cryptograms and Cryptology in American History, 1775–1900*. Vol. 1 (Ft. Meade, National Security Agency, 2002)

———. *United States Diplomatic Codes and Ciphers: 1775–1938*. (Chicago: Precedent Publishing Co., 1979)

Wills, Garry. *Inventing America: Jefferson's Declaration of Independence*. (New York: Vintage Books, 1979)

Secondary Sources: Articles

Beard, J. Howard. "The Medical Observations and Practice of Lewis and Clark" *The Scientific Monthly*. Vol. 20, No. 5 (May 1925) 506–526

Becker, Ann. "Smallpox in Washington's Army" *The Journal of Military History*. Vol. 68, No. 2 (April 2004) 381–430

Bedini, Silvio. "Thomas Jefferson: Clock Designer" *Proceedings of the American Philosophical Society*. Vol. 108, No. 3 (June 1964) 163–180

Bell, Whitfield J. "Benjamin Smith Barton, M.D. (Kiel)" *Journal of the History of Medicine and Allied Sciences*. Vol. XXVI (April 1971) 197–203

———. "A Box of Old Bones: A Note on the Identification of the Mastodon, 1766–1806" *Proceedings of the American Philosophical Society*. Vol. 93, No. 2 (May 16, 1949) 169–177

Boehm, Dwight and Edward Schwartz. "Jefferson and the Theory of Degeneracy" *American Quarterly.* Vol. 9, No. 4 (Winter 1957) 448–453

Boyd, Julian. "The Megalonyx, the Megatherium and Thomas Jefferson's Lapse of Memory" *Proceedings of the American Philosophical Society.* Vol. 102, No. 5 (October 20, 1958) 420–435

———. "Silas Deane: Death by a Kindly Teacher of Treason?" *The William and Mary Quarterly.* 3rd Series, Vol. 16, No. 2 (April 1959) 165–187

———. "Silas Deane: Death by a Kindly Teacher of Treason?" *The William and Mary Quarterly.* 3rd Series, Vol. 16, No. 3 (July 1959) 319–342

———. "Silas Deane: Death by a Kindly Teacher of Treason?" *The William and Mary Quarterly.* 3rd Series, Vol. 16, No. 4 (October 1959) 515–550

Branson, Roy. "James Madison and the Scottish Enlightenment" *Journal of the History of Ideas.* Vol. 49, No. 2 (April–June, 1979) 235–250

Brasch, Frederick. "Thomas Jefferson, the Scientist" *Science* Vol. 97, No. 2518 (April 1945) 300–301

Bronk, Detlev. "Joseph Priestley and the Early History of the American Philosophical Society" *Proceedings of the American Philosophical Society.* Vol. 86, No. 1 (September 25, 1942) 103–107

Browne, C. A. "Thomas Jefferson and Agricultural Chemistry" *The Scientific Monthly.* Vol. 60, No. 1 (January 1945) 55–62

Brown, Sanborn and Elbridge Stein. "Benjamin Thompson and the First Secret-Ink Letter of the American Revolution" *Journal of Criminal Law and Criminology.* Vol. 40, No. 5 (January–February 1950) 627–636

Brown, Sanborn and Kenneth Scott. "Count Rumford: International Informer" *The New England Quarterly.* Vol. 21, No. 1 (March 1948) 34–49

Burnett, Edmund. "Ciphers of the Revolutionary Period" *The American Historical Review.* Vol. 22, No. 2 (January 1917) 329–334

Burnstein, Andrew. "Jefferson and the Familiar Letter" *Journal of the Early Republic.* Vol. 14, No. 2 (Summer 1994) 195–220

Bushnell, David. "General Principles and Construction of a Sub-marine Vessel, communicated by D. Bushnell of Connecticut, the inventor, in a letter of October, 1787, to Thomas Jefferson then Minister Plenipotentiary of the United States at Paris" *Transactions of the American Philosophical Society.* Vol. 4, No. XXXVII (1799) 303–312

———. "The Indian Grave–A Monacan Site in Albemarle County, Virginia" *The William and Mary Quarterly.* Vol. 23, No. 2 (October 1914) 106–112

Butterfield, Lyman. "Benjamin Rush as a Promoter of Useful Knowledge" *Proceedings of the American Philosophical Society.* Vol. 92, No. 1 (March 8, 1948) 26–36

Chamberlain, Alexander. "Thomas Jefferson's Ethnological Opinions and Activities" *American Anthropologist.* Vol. 9, No. 3 (July 1907) 499–509

Chandlee, G. C. *The Scientific Monthly.* Vol. 36, No. 6 (June 1933) 568–572

Chinard, Gilbert. "Jefferson and the American Philosophical Society" *Proceedings of the American Philosophical Society.* Vol. 87, No. 3 (July 14, 1943) 263–276

Chinard, Gilbert. "The American Philosophical Society and the World of Science (1768–1800)" *Proceedings of the American Philosophical Society.* Vol. 87, No. 1 (July 14, 1943) 1–11

Church, Henry Ward. "Cornelius de Pauw and the Controversy over His Recherches Philosophiques Sur Les Americains" *PMLA.* Vol. 51, No. 1 (March 1936) 178–206

Cohen, I. Bernard. "Science and the Growth of the American Republic" *The Review of Politics*. Vol. 38, No. 3 (July 1976) 359–398

Coonen, Lester P. and Charlotte Porter. "Thomas Jefferson and American Biology" BioScience. *The Scientific Monthly*. Vol. 26, No. 12 (December 1976) 745–750

D'Elia, Donald. "Benjamin Rush, David Hartley, and the Revolutionary Uses of Psychology" *Proceedings of the American Philosophical Society*. Vol. 114, No. 2 (April 13, 1970) 109–118

———. "Jefferson, Rush, and the Limits of Philosophical Friendship" *Proceedings of the American Philosophical Society*. Vol. 117, No. 5 (October 25, 1973) 333–343

Dvoichenko-Markov, Eufronsina. "John Ledyard and the Russians." *Russian Review*. Vol. 11, No. 4 (October 1952) 211–222

Eiseley, Loren. "Indian Mythology and Extinct Fossil Vertebrates" *American Archaeologist*. New Series, Vol. 47, No. 2 (April–June 1945) 318–320

———. "Myth and Mammoth in Archaeology" *American Antiquity*. Vol. 11, No. 2 (October 1945) 84–87.

Emmons, S. F. "The Geology of Government Explorations" *Science*. Vol. 5, No. 105 (January 1, 1897) 1–15

Forman, Sidney. "Why the United States Military Academy was Established in 1802" *Military Affairs*. Vol. 29, No. 1 (Spring 1965) 16–28

———. "The United States Military Philosophical Society, 1802–1813: Scientia in Bello Pax" *The William and Mary Quarterly*. Vol. 2, No. 3 (July 1945) 273–285

"Francis Fauquier's Will." *The William and Mary Quarterly*. Vol. 8, No. 3 (January 1900) 171–177

Fraser, John A. "The Use of Encrypted, Coded and Secret Communications is an 'Ancient Liberty' Protected by the United States Constitution" *Virginia Journal of Law and Technology*. (Fall 1997)

Friis, Herman. "A Brief Review of the Development and Status of the Geographical and Cartographical Activities of the United States Government: 1776–1818" *Imago Mundi*. Vol. 19 (1965) 68–80

Furber, Louise. "Smallpox and Vaccination" *The American Journal of Nursing*. Vol. 4, No. 4 (January 1904) 257–263

Gaddy, David. "The Cylinder-Cipher" *Cryptologia*. Vol. XIX, No. 4 (October 1995) 385–391

Greenbaum, Louis. "Thomas Jefferson, the Paris Hospitals, and the University of Virginia" *Eighteenth-Century Studies*. Vol. 26, No. 4 (Summer 1993) 607–626

Greene, Jack. "Landon Carter and the Pistole Fee Dispute" *The William and Mary Quarterly*. Vol. 14, No. 1 (January 1957) 66–69

Greene, John C. "American Science Comes of Age, 1780–1820" *The Journal of American History*. Vol. 55, No. 1 (June 1968) 22–41

———. "Early Scientific Interest in the American Indian: Comparative Linguistics" *Proceedings of the American Philosophical Society*. Vol. 86, No. 1 (September 25, 1942) 511–517

———. "Science and the Public in the Age of Jefferson" *Isis*. Vol. 49, No. 1 (March 1958) 13–25

Greene, John and John G. Burke. "The Science of Minerals in the Age of Jefferson" *Transactions of the American Philosophical Society*. New Series, Vol. 68, No. 4 (1978) 1–113

Hafertepe, Kenneth. "An Inquiry into Thomas Jefferson's Ideas of Beauty" *The Journal of the Society of Architectural Historians*. Vol. 59, No. 2 (June 2000) 216–231

Hans, Nicholas. "Franklin, Jefferson, and the English Radicals at the End of the Eighteenth Century." *Proceedings of the American Philosophical Society*. Vol. 98, No. 6 (December 23, 1954) 406–426

Hantman, Jeffrey and Gary Dunham. "The Enlightened Archaeologist" *Archaeology*. Vol. 46 (May–June 1993)

Hastings, George. "Notes on the Beginnings of Aeronautics in America" *The American Historical Review*. Vol. 25, No. 1 (October 1919) 68–72

Hellman, Doris. "Jefferson's Efforts Towards the Decimalization of the United States Weights and Measures" *Isis*. Vol. 16, No. 2 (November 1931) 266–314.

Howell, Wilber S. "The Declaration of Independence and Eighteenth Century Logic" *The William and Mary Quarterly*. 3rd Series, Vol. 18, No. 4 (October 1961) 463–484

Humphreys, William. "A Review of Papers on Meteorology and Climatology Published By the American Philosophic Society Prior to the Twentieth Century" *Proceedings of the American Philosophical Society*. Vol. 86, No. 1 (September 25, 1942) 29–33

Hunt, Gaillard. "The History of the Department of State" *The American Journal of International Law*. Vol. 6, No. 4 (October 1912) 910–930

Jackson, Donald. "Ledyard and Laperouse: A Contrast in Northwestern Exploration" *The Western Historical Journal*. Vol. 9, No. 4 (October 1978) 495–508

Jefferson, Thomas and Caspar Wistar. "An Account of Two Heads Found in a Morass, Called the Big Bone Lick, and Presented to the Society, by Mr. Jefferson" *Transactions of the American Philosophical Society*. New Series, Vol.1 (1818) 375–380

Jefferson, Thomas and Rev. James Madison. "Experiments upon Magnetism communicated in a Letter to Thomas Jefferson, President of the American Philosophical Society, by the Reverend James Madison, President of William and Mary College" *Transactions of the American Philosophical Society*. Vol. IV, No. XXIX (1799) 384–390

Jones, Colin and Michael Sonenscher. "The Social Functions of the Hospital in Eighteenth-Century France: The Case of the Hôtel-Dieu of Nîmes" *French Historical Studies*. Vol. 13, No. 2 (Autumn, 1983) 172–214

Jones, William. "The Third Anniversary Discourse: On the Hindu's" *Asiatic Researches* I (1799) 422–423.

Kalman, Harold. "Newgate Prison" *Architectural History*. Vol. 12 (1969) 50–61

Kindle, E. M. "American Indian Discoveries of Vertebrate Fossils" *Journal of Paleontology*. Vol. 9, No. 5 (July 1935) 449–452

Kingsland, Lawrence. "The United States Patent Office" *Law and Contemporary Problems*. Vol. 13, No. 2 (Spring 1948) 354–367

Kiracofe, David. "Dr. Benjamin Church and the Dilemma of Treason in Revolutionary Massachusetts" *The New England Quarterly*. Vol. 70, No. 3 (September 1997) 443–462

Kramnick, Isaac. "Eighteenth-Century Science and Radical Social Theory" *The Journal of British Studies*. Vol. 25, No. 1 (January 1986) 1–30

Kruh, Louis. "The Cryptograph That Was Invented Three Times" *The Retired Officer*. (April 1971) 20–21

———. "The Genesis of the Jefferson/Bazeriers Cipher Device" *Cryptologia*. Vol. 5, No. 4 (October 1981) 193–208

Lankford, George. "Pleistocene Animals in Folk Memory" *The Journal of American Folklore*. Vol. 93, No. 369 (July–September 1980) 293–304

Macleod, Julia. "Jefferson and the Navy: A Defense" *The Huntington Library Quarterly*. Vol. 8, No. 2 (February 1945) 153–184

McKie, D. "A Note on Priestley in America" *Notes and Records of the Royal Society of London.* Vol. 10, No. 1 (October 1952) 51–59

Miller, August C. "Jefferson as an Agriculturist" *Agricultural History.* Vol. 16, No. 2 (April 1942) 65–78

Mitchell, S. A. "Astronomy during the Early Years of the American Philosophical Society" *Science.* Vol. 95, No. 2472 (May 15, 1942) 489–495

Morrell, J. B. "The University of Edinburgh in the Late Eighteenth Century: Its Scientific Eminence and Academic Structure" *Isis.* Vol. 62, No. 2 (Summer 1971) 158–171

Onuf, Peter. "The Scholars' Jefferson" *The William and Mary Quarterly.* Vol. 50, No. 4 (October 1993) 671–699

Page, John. "Memoir of Governor Page" *Virginia Historical Register and Literary Note Book.* Vol. III, No. 1 (1850) 142–151

"Papers Relating to the College" *The William and Mary Quarterly.* Vol. 16, Issue 3 (January 1908), 166–168

Pernick, Martin. "Politics, Parties, and Pestilence: Epidemic Yellow Fever in Philadelphia and the Rise of the First Party System" *The William and Mary Quarterly.* 3rd Series, Vol. 29, No. 4 (October 1972) 559–586

Peterson, Charles. "Virginia Penitentiary, 1797" *The Journal of the Society of Architectural Historians.* Vol. 12, No. 4 (December 1953) 27–28

Pickens, Buford. "Mr. Jefferson as a Revolutionary Architect" *The Journal of the Society of Architectural Historians.* Vol. 34, No. 4 (December 1975) 257–279

Preston, Richard. "The Accuracy of the Astronomical Observations of Lewis and Clark" *Proceedings of the American Philosophical Society.* Vol. 144, No. 2 (June 2000) 168–191

Randolph, Edmund. "Edmund Randolph's Essay on the Revolutionary History of Virginia" *The Virginia Magazine of History and Biography.* XLIII (1935) 120–122

Rice, Howard C. "A French Source of Jefferson's Plans for the Prison at Richmond" *The Journal of the Society of Architectural Historians.* Vol. 12, No. 4 (December 1953) 28–30.

–––. "Jefferson's Gift of Fossils to the Museum of Natural History in Paris" *Proceedings of the American Philosophical Society.* Vol. 95, No. 6 (December 1951) 597–627

Robbins, Caroline. "Honest Heretic: Joseph Priestley in America, 1794–1804" *Proceedings of the American Philosophical Society.* Vol. 106, No. 1 (February 15, 1962) 60–76

Roland, Alex. "Science and War" *Osiris.* 2nd Series, Vol. 1 (1985) 247–272

Rooney, William. "Thomas Jefferson and the New Orleans Marine Hospital" *The Journal of Southern History.* Vol. 22, No. 2 (May 1956) 167–182

Rude, G. T. "The Survey of the Continental Shelf" *The Scientific Monthly.* Vol. 34, No. 6 (June 1932) 547–550

Scott, William Berryman. "Development of American Paleontology" *Proceedings of the American Philosophical Society.* Vol. 66 (1927) 409–429

Sellers, Charles. "Unearthing the Mastodon: Peale's Greatest Triumph" *American Heritage.* Vol. 30, No. 5 (August–September 1979) 18–23

Shapley, Harlow. "Notes on Thomas Jefferson as a Natural Philosopher" *Proceedings of the American Philosophical Society.* Vol. 87, No. 3 (July 1943) 234–237

Simpson, George G. "The Beginnings of Vertebrate Paleontology in North America" *Proceedings of the American Philosophical Society.* Vol. 86, No. 1 (September 1942) 130–188

Stanton, Lucia. "A Little Matter: Jefferson's Moldboard of Least Resistance" *The Chronicle of Early American Industries Association.* Vol. 58, No. 1 (March 2005)
Stein, Susan and John Rudder. "Lighting Jefferson's Monticello" *PTB Bulletin.* Vol. 31, No. 1 (2000) 21–26
Strong, W. D. "North American Indian Traditions Suggesting a Knowledge of the Mammoth" *American Anthropologist.* Vol. 36, No. 1 (January–March 1934) 81–88
Surface, Thomas. "Thomas Jefferson: A Pioneer Student of American Geography" *Bulletin of the American Geographical Society.* Vol. 41, No. 12 (1909) 743–750
Turner, Frederick. "Jefferson to George Rogers Clark, 1783" *The American Historical Review.* Vol. 3, No. 4 (July 1898) 672–673 *The William and Mary Quarterly.* 3rd Series, Vol. 42, No. 4 (October 1955) 433–452
Wilson, M. L. "Survey of Scientific Agriculture" *Proceedings of the American Philosophical Society.* Vol. 86, No. 1 (September 1942) 52–62
Wiser, Vivian. "Weather, USDA, and the Farmer" *Agricultural History.* Vol. 63, No. 2 (September 1989) 51–61
Woods, Mary. "Thomas Jefferson and the University of Virginia: Planning the Academic Village" *The Journal of the Society of Architectural Historians.* Vol. 44, No. 3 (October 1985) 266–283.
Yochelson, Ellis. "Mr. Peale and His Mammoth Museum" *Proceedings of the American Philosophical Society.* Vol. 136, No. 4 (December 1992) 487–506

Reference Works and Newspapers

Dictionary of National Biography. (London: Smith & Elder & Co., 1908)
The Oxford Universal Dictionary. [ed.] C. T. Onions (Oxford: Clarendon Press, 1955)
Richmond Examiner. (Richmond, 1809)
Williamsburg Gazette Day Books: 1764–1766. Harrison Institute, Special Collections. The University of Virginia. Charlottesville, Virginia.

Papers

Clagett, Martin. *William Small, 1734–1775: Teacher, Mentor, Scientist.* Unpublished Ph.D. Dissertation (Richmond: Virginia Commonwealth University, 2003)
———. *James Wilson and William Small: The Scottish Connection.* Unpublished Paper. (Charlottesville: Earhart Foundation, 2007)

Endnotes

Preface

1   Keith Thomson. *Before Darwin: Reconciling God and Nature* (New Haven: Yale University Press, 2005) 40

2   Donald H Meyer. *The Democratic Enlightenment.* (New York: G.P. Putnam's Sons, 1976) 189

3   *Ibid.* 189

4   Thomas Jefferson to Peter Carr. 10 August 1787. *Jefferson Papers.* Library of Congress. Washington, D.C.

5   *Ibid.*

6   Thomas Jefferson to M. Silvestre. 29 May 1807. *Jefferson Papers.* Library of Congress. Washington, D.C.

Chapter 1: *Agriculture*

1   Thomas Jefferson to John Harvie, 14 January 1760, in *The Papers of Thomas Jefferson*, vol. 1, ed. Julian Boyd (Princeton: Princeton University Press, 1950), 3.

2   Thomas Jefferson to Pierre Samuel du Pont de Nemours, 2 March 1809, in *The Writings of Thomas Jefferson*, vol. 12, ed. Albert Bergh (Washington, D.C.: The Thomas Jefferson Memorial Foundation, 1903), 258.

3   *Thomas Jefferson's Garden Book: 1766–1824*, ed. E. Morris Betts (Charlottesville: Thomas Jefferson Memorial Foundation, 1999), 40.

4   Thomas Jefferson to David Williams, 14 November 1803, in *Jefferson Papers*, Library of Congress, Washington, D.C.

5   Thomas Jefferson to John Emmet, 2 May 1826, in *The Writings of Thomas Jefferson*, vol. 16, eds. Albert Bergh and Andrew Lipscomb (Washington, D.C.: Thomas Jefferson Memorial Association, 1903), 168–172.

6   Thomas Jefferson to John Jay, 23 August 1785, in *The Papers of Thomas Jefferson*, vol. 8, ed. Julian Boyd (Princeton: Princeton University Press, 1953), 426.

7   Thomas Jefferson to the Marquis de Lafayette, 11 April 1787, in *The Papers of Thomas Jefferson*, vol. 11, ed. Julian Boyd (Princeton: Princeton University Press, 1955), 283.

8   Thomas Jefferson to James Madison, 5 May 1793, in *The Papers of Thomas Jefferson*, vol. 26, ed. John Catanzariti (Princeton: Princeton University Press, 1995), 240.

9   Thomas Jefferson to James Madison, 19 July 1788, in *The Papers of Thomas Jefferson*, vol. 13, ed. Julian Boyd (Princeton: Princeton University Press, 1956), 379.

10   Thomas Jefferson to William Drayton, 30 July 1787, in *The Papers of Thomas Jefferson*, vol. 11, ed. Julian Boyd (Princeton: Princeton University Press, 1955), 646.

11   *Ibid.*

12   *Ibid.*, 644.

13   *Ibid.*, 645.

14   *Ibid.*, 646.

15   Thomas Jefferson to Edward Rutledge, 14 July 1787, in *The Papers of Thomas Jefferson*, vol. 11, ed. Julian Boyd (Princeton: Princeton University Press, 1955), 587.

16   Thomas Jefferson to William Drayton, 30 July 1787, in *The Papers of Thomas Jefferson*, vol. 11, ed. Julian Boyd (Princeton: Princeton University Press, 1955), 647.

17   *Ibid.*, 650.

18   *Ibid.*, 648.

19   *Ibid.*

20   Thomas Jefferson to James Ronaldson, 12 January 1813, in *The Writings of Thomas Jefferson*, vol. 13, ed. Albert Bergh (Washington, D.C.: Thomas Jefferson Memorial Association, 1903), 204.

21   *Ibid.*

22   Thomas Jefferson to Philip Mazzei, 17 March 1801, in *Works of Thomas Jefferson*, vol. 8, ed. Paul L. Ford (New York: G. P. Putnam's Sons, 1897), 15.

23   Meriwether Lewis to Thomas Jefferson, 26 March 1804, in *Jefferson Papers*, Library of Congress, Washington, D.C.

24   Thomas Jefferson to George Erving, 23 November 1809, in *The Papers of Thomas Jefferson: Retirement Series*, vol. 2, ed. Jefferson Looney (Princeton: Princeton University Press, 2005), 31.

25   Thomas Jefferson to J. Philip Reibelt, 21 December 1805, in *The Writings of Thomas Jefferson*, vol. 8, ed. Paul L. Ford (New York: G. P. Putnam's Sons, 1897), 402.

26   Joseph Dougherty to Thomas Jefferson, 15 May 1809, in *The Papers of Thomas Jefferson: Retirement Series*, vol. 2, ed. Jefferson Looney (Princeton: Princeton University Press, 2004), 199.

27   Joseph Dougherty to James Madison, 7 May 1810, Receipt, in *The Papers of James Madison: Presidential Series*, vol. 2, ed. J. C. A. Stagg (Charlottesville: University of Virginia Press, 1992), 336.

28   Thomas Jefferson to James Madison, 13 May 1810, in *The Papers of Thomas Jefferson: Retirement Series*, vol. 2, ed. Jefferson Looney (Princeton: Princeton University Press, 2005), 388.

29   *Ibid.*, 389.

30   Thomas Jefferson to Pierre Samuel du Pont de Nemours, 2 March 1809, in *Jefferson Papers*, Library of Congress, Washington, D.C.

31. Thomas Jefferson to Joseph Dougherty, 24 May 1810, in *The Papers of Thomas Jefferson: Retirement Series*, vol. 2, ed. Jefferson Looney (Princeton: Princeton University Press, 2005), 409.

32   Thomas Jefferson to William Thornton, 27 April 1810, in *Jefferson Papers*, Library of Congress, Washington, D.C.

33   Thomas Jefferson to Marquis de Lafayette, 30 November 1813, in *The Works of Thomas Jefferson*, ed. Paul Leichester Ford. (New York: Knickerbocker Press, 1903), 356

34   Silvio Bedini, *Thomas Jefferson: Statesman of Science* (New York: MacMillan, 1990), 418; Thomas Jefferson to Charles Willson Peale, 17 March 1813, in Thomas Jefferson, *The Quotable Jefferson*, ed. John Kaminski (Princeton: Princeton University Press, 2006), 8.

35   Thomas Jefferson to William Burwell, 25 February 1810, in *Jefferson Papers*, Library of Congress, Washington, D.C.

36   Thomas Jefferson to John Taylor, 29 December 1794, in *The Papers of Thomas Jefferson*, vol. 28, ed. John Catanzariti (Princeton: Princeton University Press, 2000), 231.

37   *Ibid.*, 230.

38   *Ibid.*, 231.

39   The Ha Ha fence was first suggested in 1712 in John James's *Theory and Practice of Gardening* and first employed by Royal Gardener Charles Bridgeman at Stowe in the early eighteenth century. Its intention was to create a barrier between grazing areas and gardens while providing an uninterrupted and natural view of the landscape. An additional benefit was the low cost of maintenance. The origin of its name is said to have derived from its unexpected appearance to wandering guests at Stowe; on 3 April 1786, Jefferson visited Stowe and in his account wrote,

"Within the Walk are considerable portions separated by inclosures and used for pasture. ... The inclosure is entirely by ha! ha! They are seen from one the other, the line of sight passing, not thro' the garden, but through the country parallel to the line of the garden. This has a good effect." *The Papers of Thomas Jefferson*, vol. 9, ed. Julian Boyd (Princeton: Princeton University Press, 1954), 371.

40   Jefferson's Notes on the Hessian Fly, in *The Papers of Thomas Jefferson*, vol. 20, ed. Julian Boyd (Princeton: Princeton University Press, 1982), 456.

41   Thomas Jefferson to Thomas Mann Randolph, 1 May 1791, in *The Papers of Thomas Jefferson*, vol. 20, ed. Julian Boyd (Princeton: Princeton University Press, 1982), 341.

42   "Bartram ... promises to shew me the insect this summer." Thomas Jefferson to Thomas Mann Randolph, 1 May 1791, in *The Papers of Thomas Jefferson*, vol. 20, ed. Julian Boyd (Princeton: Princeton University Press, 1982), 341.

43   Jefferson's Notes on the Hessian Fly, 461n.

44   *Ibid.*, 457.

45   Thomas Jefferson to Thomas Mann Randolph, 1 May 1791, in *The Papers of Thomas Jefferson*, vol. 20, ed. Julian Boyd (Princeton: Princeton University Press, 1982), 341.

46   Thomas Jefferson to James Adair, 1 September 1793, in *The Papers of Thomas Jefferson*, vol. 27, ed. John Catanzariti (Princeton: Princeton University Press, 1997), 3.

47   *Ibid.*

48   *Ibid.*

49   Thomas Jefferson to James Madison, 5 May 1793, *The Papers of Thomas Jefferson*, vol. 25, ed. John Catanzariti (Princeton: Princeton University Press, 1992), 660.

50   *Ibid.*

51   Thomas Jefferson to James Adair, 1 September 1793, in *The Papers of Thomas Jefferson*, vol. 27, ed. John Catanzariti (Princeton: Princeton University Press, 1997), 3.

52   Thomas Jefferson to Charles Willson Peale, 8 May 1816, in *Jefferson Papers*, Library of Congress, Washington, D.C.

53   Thomas Jefferson, Tour through Holland, in *The Papers of Thomas Jefferson*, vol. 13, ed. Julian Boyd (Princeton: Princeton University Press, 1956), 26.

54   Lucia Stanton, "A Little Matter: Jefferson's Moldboard of Least Resistance," *The Chronicle of the Early American Industries Association* 58, no. 1 (March 2005): 11n19.

55   Thomas Jefferson to Sir John Sinclair, 23 March 1798, in *The Papers of Thomas Jefferson*, vol. 30, ed. Barbara Oberg (Princeton: Princeton University Press, 2002), 199.

56   Thomas Jefferson to John Taylor, 29 December 1794, in *Jefferson Papers*, Library of Congress, Washington, D.C.

57   Stanton, "Jefferson's Moldboard," 5; Thomas Jefferson to John Sinclair, 23 March 1798, in *Jefferson Papers*, Library of Congress, Washington, D.C.

58   Thomas Jefferson to Jonathan Williams, 3 July 1796, in *The Papers of Thomas Jefferson*, vol. 29, ed. Barbara Oberg (Princeton: Princeton University Press, 2002), 140.

59   Thomas Jefferson to Sir John Sinclair, 23 March 1798, in *The Papers of Thomas Jefferson*, vol. 30, ed. Barbara Oberg (Princeton: Princeton University Press, 2002), 199. The part of this letter dealing with the moldboard plough was printed in the *Transactions of the American Philosophical Society* 4, no. XXXVIII (1799): 313–322, under the title "The description of a Mould-board of the least resistence, & of the easiest and most certain construction, taken from a letter to Sir John Sinclair, President of the board of agriculture at London."

60   Stanton, "Jefferson's Moldboard," 7.

61   *Ibid.*, 6.

62   *Ibid.*; David Baillie to Thomas Jefferson, 21 October 1807, in *Thomas Jefferson's Farm Book*, ed. Edwin Betts (Princeton, NJ: Princeton University Press, 1953), 57.

63   Stanton, "Jefferson's Moldboard," 5.

64   *Ibid.*, 10.

65   Jefferson wrote to Charles Willson Peale on March 21, 1815, informing him that he has "an iron mould board so light that it required only two small horses and it does beautiful work and is approved by everyone." *The Papers of Thomas Jefferson*, vol. 30, ed. Barbara Oberg (Princeton: Princeton University Press, 2002), 208n.

66   Stanton, "Jefferson's Moldboard," 9.

Chapter 2: *Archaeology, Anthropology, Ethnology, and Comparative Linguistics*

1   Bernard W. Sheehan, *Seeds of Extinction* (Chapel Hill: University of North Carolina Press, 1973), 68.

2   *Ibid.*, 70.

3   Thomas Jefferson, "Autobiography," in *The Life and Selected Writings of Thomas Jefferson*, ed. Adrienne Koch and William Peden (New York: Random House, 1943), 63.

4   Peter S. Onuf, *Jefferson's Empire* (Charlottesville: University of Virginia Press, 2000), 18.

5   Sheehan, *Seeds*, 59.

6   Anthony F. C. Wallace, *Jefferson and the Indians* (Cambridge: Belknap Press, 1999), 158.

7   *Ibid.*, 137.

8   Thomas Jefferson to Edward Rutledge, 18 July 1788, in *The Papers of Thomas Jefferson*, vol. 13, ed. Julian Boyd (Princeton: Princeton University Press, 1956), 377.

9   Sheehan, *Seeds*, 60.

10 Wallace, *Jefferson and the Indians*, 130.

11 Sheehan, *Seeds*, 60.

12 Thomas Jefferson to Ezra Stiles, 1 September 1786, in *The Papers of Thomas Jefferson*, vol. 10, ed. Julian Boyd (Princeton: Princeton University Press, 1954), 316.

13 John Ledyard to Thomas Jefferson, 29 July 1787, in *The Papers of Thomas Jefferson*, vol. 11, ed. Julian Boyd (Princeton: Princeton University Press, 1955), 638. Ledyard may have been an agent for Jefferson. He was ejected from Russia as a spy. Jefferson wrote to Charles Thomson about Ledyard, "He is a person of ingenuity and information. Unfortunately, he has too much imagination. However, if he escapes successfully, he will give us new, various, and useful information." Thomas Jefferson to Charles Thomson, 20 September 1787, in *The Papers of Thomas Jefferson*, vol. 12, ed. Julian Boyd (Princeton: Princeton University Press, 1955), 160.

14 C. W. Ceram, *The First American: A Story of North American Archaeology* (New York: Harcourt Brace Jovanovich, 1972), 4.

15 *Ibid.*

16 Jeffrey Hantman and Gary Dunham, "The Enlightened Archaeologist," *Archaeology* vol. 46 (May–June 1993), 46.

17 Sir Robert Eric Mortimer Wheeler (1890–1976), born in Glasgow, was most influential in Indian archaeology. He was honored repeatedly for his achievements, he was director of the National Museum of Wales (1920), keeper of the archaeological department of the National Museum in Wales (1926–44), lecturer in archaeology at the University College of Cardiff, director general of archaeology in India (1944–47), archaeological advisor to the Pakistani National Museum, and professor of Roman archaeology at the University of London (1948–55). Wheeler carried out important excavations in Britain at Verulamium and Maiden Castle and was knighted in 1952.

18 Ceram, *First American*, 9. Actual date of excavation c. 1780/1781.

19 Thomas Jefferson, *Notes on the State of Virginia*, ed. William Peden (Chapel Hill: University of North Carolina Press, 1995), 98.

20 Ceram, *First American*, 107.

21 Jefferson, *State of Virginia*, 99.

22 *Ibid.*

23 Ceram, *First American*, 8.

24 Jefferson, *State of Virginia*, 100.

25 Hantman and Dunham, "Enlightened Archaeologist," 47.

26 Harry Innes to Thomas Jefferson, 8 July 1790, in *The Papers of Thomas Jefferson*, vol. 17, ed. Julian Boyd (Princeton: Princeton University Press, 1965), 20.

27 Wallace, *Jefferson and the Indians*, 139.

28 Thomas Jefferson to Henry Brackenridge, 20 September 1813, in *Jefferson Papers*, Library of Congress, Washington, D.C.

29 *The Oxford Universal Dictionary*, ed. C. T. Onions (Oxford: Clarendon Press, 1955), Anthropology, 74; Ethnogeny and Ethnology, 637.

30 John Ledyard to Thomas Jefferson, 7 February 1786, in *The Papers of Thomas Jefferson*, vol. 9, ed. Julian Boyd (Princeton: Princeton University Press, 1954), 261n.

31 John Ledyard to Thomas Jefferson, 3 July 1788, in *The Papers of Thomas Jefferson*, vol. 13, ed. Julian Boyd (Princeton: Princeton University Press, 1956), 306.

32 Wallace, *Jefferson and the Indians*, 111.

33 *Ibid.*, 112.

34 *Ibid.*

35 *Ibid.*, 113.

36 *Ibid.*

37 *Ibid.*, 116.

38 *Ibid.*, 119.

39 *Ibid.*, 171.

40 John Adams to Thomas Jefferson, 28 June 1813, Bergh. 13 (285), in Wallace, *Jefferson and the Indians*, 129.

41 Robert Bieder, *Science Encounters the Indian, 1820–1880* (Norman: University of Oklahoma Press, 1986), 37.

42 Thomas Jefferson to André Michaux, 23 January 1793, in *The Papers of Thomas Jefferson*, vol. 25, ed. John Catanzariti (Princeton: Princeton University Press, 1992), 81.

43 *Ibid.*

44 Thomas Jefferson to Meriwether Lewis, 20 June 1803, Instructions, in *Jefferson Papers*, Library of Congress, Washington, D.C.

45 Jefferson, *State of Virginia*, 101.

46 William Jones, "The Third Anniversary Discourse: On the Hindus," *Asiatic Researches* 1 (1799): 422–23, in Edward Gray, *New World Babel* (Princeton: Princeton University Press, 1999), 117.

47 Gray, *New World Babel*, 117.

48 *Ibid.*

49 *Ibid.*, 118.

50 *Ibid.*, 126.

51 Wallace, *Jefferson and the Indians*, 146.

52 Jefferson, *State of Virginia*, 101.

53 "Hawkins had been a member, along with Jefferson, of the committee of the Continental Congress overseeing Indian Affairs, and in 1785 he was one of the commissioners to negotiate treaties of peace and settle boundary questions with the southern tribes." Wallace, *Jefferson and the Indians*, 119; "I begin by inclosing you a geographical and statistical account in MS of the Creek or Muscogee Indians and country as it was in the years 98 and 99. this written by Col. Hawkins who has lived among them as an agent now upwards of 20. years." Thomas Jefferson to Stephen du Poinceau, 22 January 1816, in *Jefferson Papers*, Library of Congress, Washington, D.C.

54 Thomas Jefferson to Benjamin Hawkins, 13 August 1786, in *The Papers of Thomas Jefferson*, vol. 10, ed. Julian Boyd (Princeton: Princeton University Press, 1954), 240.

55 Thomas Jefferson to Benjamin Hawkins, 14 March 1800, in *The Papers of Thomas Jefferson*, vol. 14, ed. Barbara Oberg (Princeton: Princeton University Press, 2004), 436.

56. Wallace, *Jefferson and the Indians*, 147.

57 *Ibid.*, 150.

58 Class 497, no. J35, library, American Philosophical Society, Philadelphia, PA.

59 Jefferson, *State of Virginia*, 102.

60 Gray, *New World Babel*, 130.

61 Thomas Jefferson to Benjamin Smith Barton, 21 September 1809, in *The Papers of Thomas Jefferson: Retirement Series*, vol. 1, ed. Jefferson Looney (Princeton: Princeton University Press, 2004), 556.

62 *Ibid.* The trunk was in transit from Washington, D.C. to Richmond when it disappeared in early spring 1809. Jefferson reported, "my trunk No 28. may have miscarried. ... It is a hair trunk, square, of about 6. or 7. feet cubic contents, & very heavy. ... It contained a pocket telescope of 5. guineas sterling cost, a Dynometer just received from France of 4. guineas, and other things which I do not recollect." Optimistically he concluded, "I am still in hopes that a conference between mr Randolph's boatmen & the drayman may trace it to it's deposit—perhaps it may have been mis-delivered." Thomas Jefferson to George Jefferson, 1 May 1809, in *The Papers of*

Thomas Jefferson: Retirement Series, vol. 1, ed. Jefferson Looney (Princeton: Princeton University Press, 2004), 180. His anxiety increased because he realized that among the possessions was a pocket telescope with a brass case, a Dynometer of steel and brass for measuring the exertions of draught animals and the only one in America, and, most importantly, a collection of vocabularies of the Indian languages. He instructed George Jefferson to offer a reward "what you think proper under 20. or 30. Dollars" and estimated the true value of the contents of the trunk to be about 150. "Dollars exclusive of the Vocabularies, which had been the labour of 30 years in collection for publication." Thomas Jefferson to George Jefferson, 18 May 1809, in *The Papers of Thomas Jefferson: Retirement Series*, vol. 1, ed. Jefferson Looney (Princeton: Princeton University Press, 2004), 204. Toward the end of June, George Jefferson wrote to Jefferson that "our lost trunk is in the possession of one Dan Northcut" of Lynchburg who "purchased the contents of the trunk with its contents from a negro waterman for 3$!" However, Northcut reported that there was some writing which he did not understand, giving hope that "the vocabularies of the indian languages are not all destroyed." George Jefferson to Thomas Jefferson, 26 June 1809, in *The Papers of Thomas Jefferson: Retirement Series*, vol. 1, ed. Jefferson Looney (Princeton: Princeton University Press, 2004), 311. Sam Harrison, an agent engaged by George Jefferson to recover the trunk, wrote, "I believe that we have got the Thief; by the name of Ned, the property of James B. Couch Dec.d late of Buckingham County. ... Ned is a Noted Villain, & from testimony here ... he Brocke the Trunk open ... Took Such of the Articles as he thought would be of Service to him ... [and] Threw it, with the Balance of the articles overboard, just below Britains Landing, nearly opposite westham." Ned acknowledged to his fellow boatmen that he had stolen the trunk and was found in possession of a bag with Mr. Jefferson's name. The discarded trunk was subsequently found by white boatmen, "who declare there was nothing [left], but paper, & papers; that they were Chiefly wet; & many of them were out of the Trunk, & perhaps 100 yards Distant." The boatmen thereupon separated the papers and spread them out in the boat for several days to dry. Samuel J. Harrison to Gibson and Jefferson, 16 July 1809, in *The Papers of Thomas Jefferson: Retirement Series*, vol. 1, ed. Jefferson Looney (Princeton: Princeton University Press, 2004), 346–347. For the theft of Jefferson's trunk, Mr. Couch's Ned was found guilty of a felony on 25 July 1809 and was sentenced to "be burnt in his left hand and receive thirty-nine lashes on his bare back at the public whipping post." *The Papers of Thomas Jefferson: Retirement Series*, vol. 1, ed. Jefferson Looney (Princeton: Princeton University Press, 2004), 348n.

CHAPTER 3: *Paleontology*

1   Silvio Bedini, *Thomas Jefferson and American Vertebrate Paleontology* (Charlottesville: Commonwealth of Virginia, 1985), 1; Gilbert Chinard, *Thomas Jefferson: Apostle of Americanism* (Boston: Little, Brown and Co., 1929), 118.

2   William Berryman Scott, "Development of American Paleontology," *Proceedings of the American Philosophical Society*, vol. 66 (1927), 410. Jefferson's preeminence was denied by Scott on the contention that the possibility of extinction was a *sine qua non* for true paleontological discourse. "The paleontology of the vertebrates may be said to date from 1796, when Cuvier demonstrated that the fossil elephants of France and Italy did not belong to any existing species." [Actually, Cuvier's identification was based upon the reexamination of the Ohio fossils from the Morgan collection remains by Adrian Camper and Prof. Johann H. F. Authenrieth and by the drawings of Charles Willson Peale. Whitfield J. Bell, "A Box of Old Bones: A Note on the Identification of the Mastodon, 1766–1806," *Proceedings of the American Philosophical Society*, vol. 93, no. 2 (May 16, 1949), 177.] William Hunter had reached the same conclusion—"its whole generation is probably extinct"—nearly thirty years before Cuvier (1768). George G. Simpson, "The Beginnings of Vertebrate Paleontology in North America," *Proceedings of the American Philosophical Society*, vol. 86, no. 1 (September 25, 1942), 149. Also "On April 3, 1789, the Reverend Dr. Nicholas Collin read to the American Philosophical Society ... the vast Mahmot is perhaps yet stalking through the western wilderness; but if he is no more, let us carefully gather his remains" (*Ibid.*, 130). "In the long roster of American vertebrate paleontologists, the name Casper Wistar should stand first in time. ... It is ironic that the traditions of later vertebrate paleontology should have transferred to Jefferson much of the credit that Jefferson, himself, rightly granted to Wistar" (*Ibid.*, 153). The first objection of Scott to Jefferson's right to the title "Father of American Vertebrate Paleontology" is predicated on the requisite and absolute belief that the species of mammoth was extinct at the time of the investigations; the second objection of Simpson that Jefferson himself credited Wistar as preeminent in the field—Jefferson in a consistent manner and in all fields modestly played down his own abilities and deferred preeminence to a colleague.

3   George G. Simpson, "The Beginnings of Vertebrate Paleontology in North America," *Proceedings of the American Philosophical Society*, vol. 86, no. 1 (September 25, 1942), 133.

4   *Ibid.*

5   *Ibid.*

6   *Ibid.*, 132.

7   *Ibid.*, 134.

8   Mark Catesby, *The Natural History of Carolina, Florida and the Bahama Islands*, vol. II (London, 1743), appendix, vii, as quoted in Simpson, "Beginnings of Vertebrate Paleontology," 134.

9   Simpson, "Beginnings of Vertebrate Paleontology," 137.

10   Whitfield J. Bell, "A Box of Old Bones: A Note on the Identification of the Mastodon, 1766–1806," *Proceedings of the American Philosophical Society*, vol. 93, no. 2 (May 16, 1949), 169.

11   *Ibid.*, 170.

12   MSS, 21648 (333–334), British Museum, as quoted in Simpson, "Beginnings of Vertebrate Paleontology." 140.

13   *Ibid.*

14   *Ibid.*

15   *Dictionary of American Biography*, vol. IV, ed. Albert Volwiler (556–557), as quoted in Simpson, "Beginnings of Vertebrate Paleontology," 142.

16   *Ibid.*

17   Simpson, "Beginnings of Vertebrate Paleontology," 142.

18   *Ibid.*, 149.

19   Thomas Jefferson to John Stuart, 10 November 1796, *The Papers of Thomas Jefferson*, vol. 29, ed. Barbara Oberg (Princeton: Princeton University Press, 2002), 206.

20   Bell, "A Box of Old Bones," 172; Robert Annan, "Account of a skeleton of a large animal, found near Hudson's river," *Memoirs American Academy of Arts and Sciences*, vol. 2 (1793), 160–164; See Martin Clagett, *The Scottish Years of James Wilson and William Small*, unpublished manuscript (Williamsburg: Earhart Foundation, 2007); Robert Annan to Bird Wilson, 16 May 1805. *Montgomery Collection*, Pennsylvania Historical Society. Philadelphia, PA.

21   Bell, "A Box of Old Bones," 173.

22   Simpson, "Beginnings of Vertebrate Paleontology," 156.

23   John Stuart to Thomas Jefferson, 11 April 1796, in *The Papers of Thomas Jefferson*, vol. 29, ed. Barbara Oberg (Princeton: Princeton University Press, 2002), 64.

24   Julian P. Boyd, "The Megalonyx, the Megatherium and Thomas Jefferson's Lapse of Memory," *Proceedings of the American Philosophical Society*, vol. 102, no. 5 (October 20, 1958), 422; Thomas Jefferson to Archibald Stuart, 26 May 1796, in *The Papers of Thomas Jefferson*, vol. 29, ed. Barbara Oberg (Princeton: Princeton University Press, 2002), 113.

25   John Stuart to Thomas Jefferson, 13 July 1796, in *The Papers of Thomas Jefferson*, vol. 29, ed. Barbara Oberg (Princeton: Princeton University Press, 2002), 152.

26   *Ibid.*

27   Philip Turpin to Thomas Jefferson, 18 July 1796, in *The Papers of Thomas Jefferson*, vol. 29, ed. Barbara Oberg (Princeton: Princeton University Press, 2002), 155.

28   Boyd, "Megalonyx, Megatherium, Memory," 422; Thomas Jefferson to David Rittenhouse, 3 July 1796, *The Papers of Thomas Jefferson*, vol. 29, ed. Barbara Oberg (Princeton: Princeton University Press, 2002), 138.

29   Boyd, "Megalonyx, Megatherium, Memory," 422; Thomas Jefferson to David Rittenhouse, 3 July 1796, *The Papers of Thomas Jefferson*, vol. 29, ed. Barbara Oberg (Princeton: Princeton University Press, 2002), 138.

30   Benjamin Smith Barton to Thomas Jefferson, 1 August 1796, in *The Papers of Thomas Jefferson*, vol. 29, ed. Barbara Oberg (Princeton: Princeton University Press, 2002), 165.

31   *Ibid.*

32   Thomas Jefferson to Benjamin Smith Barton, 10 October 1796, in *The Papers of Thomas Jefferson*, vol. 29, ed. Barbara Oberg (Princeton: Princeton University Press, 2002), 192. John Stuart wrote in January 1797 that a thighbone had actually been found in the cave "but by some unaccountable reason it is mislayed that it cannot be found again." John Stuart to Thomas Jefferson, 16 January 1797, in *The Papers of Thomas Jefferson*, vol. 29, ed. Barbara Oberg (Princeton: Princeton University Press, 2002), 266.

33   Thomas Jefferson to Benjamin Smith Barton, 10 October 1796, in *The Papers of Thomas Jefferson*, vol. 29, ed. Barbara Oberg (Princeton: Princeton University Press, 2002), 192.

34 Thomas Jefferson to Benjamin Rush, 22 January 1797, in *The Papers of Thomas Jefferson*, vol. 29, ed. Barbara Oberg (Princeton: Princeton University Press, 2002), 275.

35 Thomas Jefferson to the American Philosophical Society, 28 January 1797, in *The Papers of Thomas Jefferson*, vol. 29, ed. Barbara Oberg (Princeton: Princeton University Press, 2002), 192.

36 Thomas Jefferson to Benjamin Rush, 22 January 1797, in *The Papers of Thomas Jefferson*, vol. 29, ed. Barbara Oberg (Princeton: Princeton University Press, 2002), 275.

37 Benjamin Rush to Thomas Jefferson, 4 February 1797, *The Papers of Thomas Jefferson*, vol. 29, ed. Barbara Oberg (Princeton: Princeton University Press, 2002), 284.

38 *Ibid.*

39 The nascent and shocking theory of the evolution of the species did not begin with Charles Darwin but rather with his grandfather Erasmus Darwin, his friends in the Birmingham Lunar Circle, colleagues from the Universities of Glasgow and Edinburgh, and scholars at Marischal College. The first geological indications appeared in the Derbyshire ramblings of Darwin, Small, and Hutton. See Jenny Uglow. *The Lunar Men* (London: Farrar, Straus and Giroux, 2002)

40 Boyd, "Megalonyx, Megatherium, and Memory," 425.

41 Silvio Bedini, *Thomas Jefferson: Statesman of Science* (New York: Macmillan, 1990), 270.

42 The Real Gabinete de Historia Natural was founded by Charles III in 1771. From its inception Charles had issued orders that all Intendents of Provinces and Viceroys of Colonies should instruct clergy to search for objects of interest to natural history and send whatever contributions forth to Madrid. The director of the museum was Juan Baptista Bru y Ramon, who was both a gifted author and an illustrator.

43 Boyd, "Megalonyx, Megatherium, Memory," 426.

44 Bedini, *Vertebrate Paleontology*, 10.

45 William Carmichael to Thomas Jefferson, 26 January 1789, in *The Papers of Thomas Jefferson*, vol. 14, ed. Julian Boyd (Princeton: Princeton University Press, 1958), 504 enclosure.

46 *Ibid.*

47 *Ibid.*

48 *Ibid.*

49 Thomas Jefferson to William Carmichael, 8 May 1789, in *The Papers of Thomas Jefferson*, vol. 15, ed. Julian Boyd (Princeton: Princeton University Press, 1958), 103. "Your favor of Jan. 26. & Mar. 27. is duly recieved and I thank you for the interesting papers it contained."

50 Boyd, "Megalonyx, Megatherium, Memory," 434.

51 Bedini, *Statesman*, 274.

52 *Ibid.*, 281.

53 Thomas Jefferson to Robert Livingston, 14 December 1800, in *The Papers of Thomas Jefferson*, vol. 32, ed. Barbara Oberg (Princeton: Princeton University Press, 2005), 302.

54 Robert Livingston to Thomas Jefferson, 7 January 1801, in *The Papers of Thomas Jefferson*, vol. 32, ed. Barbara Oberg (Princeton: Princeton University Press, 2005), 406; see also Thomas Jefferson to Caspar Wistar, 3 February 1801, in Archives, Clermont State Historical Site, Germantown, New York, Cl.1987, 32.A. B. (LFP/Box 82/Folder 07). Courtesy of Donald Fraser and Kjirsten Gustavson of the Clermont State Historical Site.

55 Robert Livingston to Thomas Jefferson, 7 January 1801, in *The Papers of Thomas Jefferson*, vol. 32, ed. Barbara Oberg (Princeton: Princeton University Press, 2005) 407; see also Thomas Jefferson to Caspar Wistar, 3 February 1801, in Archives, Clermont State Historical Site, Germantown, New York. Cl.1987, 32.A. B. (LFP/Box 82/Folder 07). Courtesy of Donald Fraser and Kjirsten Gustavson of the Clermont State Historical Site.

56 Robert Livingston to Thomas Jefferson, 7 January 1801, in *The Papers of Thomas Jefferson*, vol. 32, ed. Barbara Oberg (Princeton: Princeton University Press, 2005), 407; *see also* Thomas Jefferson to Caspar Wistar, 3 February 1801, Archives, Clermont State Historical Site, Germantown, New York. Cl.1987, 32.A. B. (LFP/Box 82/Folder 07). Courtesy of Donald Fraser and Kjirsten Gustavson of the Clermont State Historical Site.

57 Charles C. Sellers, "Unearthing the Mastodon," *American Heritage* (August - September 1979), 18.

58 *Ibid.*

59 *Ibid.*

60 *Ibid.*, 19.

61   Ellis Yochelson, "Mr. Peale and His Mammoth Museum," *Proceedings of the American Philosophical Society*, vol. 136, no. 4 (December 1992), 496; Sellers, "Unearthing the Mastodon," 19. Peale constructed "a huge mill wheel, powered not by water flowing over the outside but by men walking within." Peale estimated that he could remove "1440 Gallns. Pr. Hour with the labour of 3 men."

62   Bedini, *Statesman*, 342.

63   Sellers, "Unearthing the Mastodon," 22.

64   *Ibid.*, 23.

65   Ellis Yochelson, "Mr. Peale and His Mammoth Museum," *Proceedings of the American Philosophical Society*, vol. 136, no. 4 (December 1992), 497.

66   Bedini, *Statesman*, 342.

67   Thomas Jefferson to Meriwether Lewis, June 20, 1803, Instructions, in *Writings*, ed. Merrill Peterson (New York: Viking Press, 1984), 1127. "Your observations are to be taken with great pains & accuracy, to be entered distinctly & intelligibly for others, as well as yourself, to comprehend all the elements necessary, with the aid of the usual tables, to fix the latitude and longitude of the places at which they were taken, and are to be rendered to the war office for the purpose of having the calculations made concurrently by proper persons within the US. several copies of these as well as of your other notes should be made at leisure times, & put into the care of the most trust-worthy of your attendants, to guard by multiplying them against the accidental losses to which they will be exposed. A further guard would be that one these copies be on the paper of the birch, as less liable to injury from damp than common paper."

68   *Ibid.*, 1128. "The mineral productions of every kind; but more particularly metals; limestone, pit-coal, & salt-petre; salines & mineral waters, noting the temperature of the last & such circumstances as may indicate their character."

69   *Ibid.* "And considering the interest which every nation has in extending & strengthening the authority of reason & justice among the people around them, it will be useful to acquire what knolege you can of the state of morality, religion, & information among them; as it may better enable those who may endeavor to civilize & instruct them, to adapt their measures to the existing notions & practices of those on whom they are to operate."

70   *Ibid.* "Climate, as characterized by the thermometer, by the proportion of rainy, cloudy, & clear days, by lightening, hail, snow, ice, by the access & recess of frost, by the winds prevailing at different seasons, the dates at which particular plants put forth or lose their flower, or leaf, times of appearance of particular birds, reptiles or insects."

71   Bedini, *Statesman*, 370.

72   *Ibid.*, 371.

73   *Ibid.*, 372.

74   Thomas Jefferson to Charles Willson Peale, 5 May 1809, in *The Papers of Thomas Jefferson: Retirement Series*, ed. Jefferson Looney (Princeton: Princeton University Press, 2005), 187.

75   Caspar Wistar to Thomas Jefferson, 30 August 1808, in *Jefferson Papers*, Library of Congress, Washington, D.C. In the same year that Blumenbach named the mammoth, a hunter discovered one entombed in permafrost in a bank of the Lena River, Siberia. Over the next few years, thawing freed enough of the carcass from the ice that the hunter was able to remove the tusks, which he sold to a merchant in the city of Yakust. In 1806 Mikhail (Michael) Adams, a Scottish botanist attached to the Russian Academy of Science, received word of the mammoth while traveling through Yakust. When his party reached it, they found a badly decomposed carcass. However, it still had considerable patches of skin and hair and most of the skeleton was intact. The find was transported to St. Petersburg, where it was mounted at the Zoological Institute. It became known as the Adams mammoth.

76   Thomas Jefferson to William Brown, 10 September 1809, in *The Papers of Thomas Jefferson: Retirement Series*, ed. Jefferson Looney (Princeton: Princeton University Press, 2005), 509.

77   Thomas Jefferson to William Clark, 10 September 1809, in *The Papers of Thomas Jefferson: Retirement Series*, ed. Jefferson Looney (Princeton: Princeton University Press, 2005), 510.

78   *Ibid.*

79   Bedini, *Vertebrate Paleontology*, 17.

80   *Ibid.*, 23.

CHAPTER 4: *Social Architecture and Public Health*

1   Louise Furber, "Smallpox and Vaccination," *The American Journal of Nursing* 4, no. 4 (January 1904): 259.

2   *Ibid.*

3   Francis Fauquier received the honor posthumously.

4   Benjamin Franklin and William Heberden, *Some Account of the Success of Inoculation for the Small-Pox in England and America* (London: William Strahan, 1759). William Heberden was a well-known and respected London physician with connections to William Small, Alexander Small, Erasmus Darwin, Sir John Pringle, John Fordyce, William Hunter, and other medical luminaries of the late 18th century. He advocated and obtained a post at the Royal Court of Russia in St. Petersburg for William Small in 1765; Small declined.

5   *Ibid.*, 3.

6   *Ibid.*, 4.

7   *Ibid.*

8   *Ibid.*

9   *Ibid.*

10   *Ibid.*, 5.

11   George Gilmer to John Morgan, 11 May 1766, in *The Papers of Thomas Jefferson*, vol. 1, ed. Julian Boyd (Princeton: Princeton University Press, 1950), 18. George Gilmer was in Jefferson's class at the College of William and Mary studying with William Small. *Vide*, "The Faculty and Alumni of the College of William and Mary," Special Collections, College of William and Mary, Williamsburg, Va. It is likely that Small encouraged Gilmer, McClurg, and Walter Jones to study at Edinburgh where his old mentor, John Gregory, was mediciner.

12   Silvio Bedini, *Thomas Jefferson: Statesman of Science* (New York: Macmillan, 1990), 46.

13   Robert Halsey, *How the President, Thomas Jefferson, and Doctor Benjamin Waterhouse Established Vaccination as a Public Health Procedure* (New York: New York Academy of Medicine, 1936), 3.

14   *Ibid.*, 11.

15   Benjamin Waterhouse to Reverend Timothy Dwight, 23 March 1801, in Robert Halsey, *How the President, Thomas Jefferson, and Doctor Benjamin Waterhouse Established Vaccination as a Public Health Procedure* (New York: New York Academy of Medicine, 1936), 24.

16   Halsey, *Vaccination as Public Health Procedure*, 25.

17   *Ibid.*, 16.

18   Benjamin Waterhouse to Thomas Jefferson, 1 December 1800, in *The Papers of Thomas Jefferson*, vol. 32, ed. Barbara Oberg (Princeton: Princeton University Press, 2005), 264; Enclosure in Benjamin Waterhouse, "A Prospect of Exterminating the Small-Pox; Being the History of the Variolae Vaccinae, or Kine-Pox, Commonly Called Cow-Pox" (Cambridge, 1800); Sowerby, no. 945, *The Papers of Thomas Jefferson*, vol. 32, ed. Barbara Oberg (Princeton: Princeton University Press, 2005), 264n.

19   Thomas Jefferson to Benjamin Waterhouse, 25 December 1800, in *The Papers of Thomas Jefferson*, vol. 32, ed. Barbara Oberg (Princeton: Princeton University Press, 2005), 355.

20   Thomas Jefferson to Benjamin Waterhouse, 25 July 1801, in Halsey, *Vaccination as Public Health Procedure*, 31, Library of Congress.

21   *Ibid.*

22   John Shore to Thomas Jefferson, 1 August 1801, in Halsey, *Vaccination as Public Health Procedure*, 32, Library of Congress.

23   Thomas Jefferson to Benjamin Waterhouse, 8 August 1801, in Halsey, *Vaccination as Public Health Procedure*, 32, Library of Congress.

24   Thomas Jefferson to Benjamin Waterhouse, 14 August 1801, in Halsey, *Vaccination as Public Health Procedure*, 34, Library of Congress.

25   Thomas Jefferson to Benjamin Waterhouse, 21 August 1801, in Halsey, *Vaccination as Public Health Procedure*, 35, Library of Congress.

26   Benjamin Waterhouse to Thomas Jefferson, 2 September 1801, in Halsey, *Vaccination as Public Health Procedure*, 38, Library of Congress.

27   *Ibid.*

28   Thomas Jeffferson to John Shore, 12 September 1801, in Halsey, *Vaccination as Public Health Procedure*, 39, Massachusetts Historical Society.

29   Benjamin Waterhouse to John Gantt, 11 January 1802, in Halsey, *Vaccination as Public Health Procedure*, 50.

30   Thomas Jefferson to Meriwether Lewis, "Instructions to Captain Lewis," 20 June 1803, in *Thomas Jefferson: Writings*, ed. Merrill Peterson (New York: Literary Classics of the United States, 1984), 1130.

31   Martin Pernick, "Politics, Parties, and Pestilence: Epidemic Yellow Fever in Philadelphia and the Rise of the First Party System," *William and Mary Quarterly*, 3rd ser., vol. 29, no. 4 (October 1972): 559.

32   "The Anglican party is busy as you may suppose in making the worst of every thing, and in turning public feelings against France, and thence, in favor of England." James Madison to Thomas Jefferson. 2 September 1793, in *The Papers of Thomas Jefferson*, vol. 27, ed. John Catazariti (Princeton: Princeton University Press, 1997), 16.

33   Pernick, "Politics, Parties, Pestilence," 559.

34   *Ibid.*, 568.

35   *Ibid.*, 559.

36   Thomas Jefferson to Thomas Mann Randolph, Jr., 2 September 1793, in *The Papers of Thomas Jefferson*, vol. 27, ed. John Catazariti (Princeton: Princeton University Press, 1997), 21.

37   *Ibid.*

38   Thomas Jefferson to Thomas Pinckney, 27 November 1793, in *The Papers of Thomas Jefferson*, vol. 27, ed. John Catazariti (Princeton: Princeton University Press, 1997), 450.

39   *Ibid.*

40   Thomas Jefferson to John Page, 16 August 1804, in *Jefferson Papers*, Library of Congress, Washington, D.C.

41   *Ibid.*

42   Thomas Jefferson to Count de Volney, 8 February 1805, in *Jefferson Papers*, Library of Congress, Washington, D.C.

43   Thomas Jefferson to Benjamin Rush, 23 September 1800, in *The Papers of Thomas Jefferson*, vol. 32, ed. Barbara Oberg (Princeton: Princeton University Press, 2005), 166.

44   Thomas Jefferson to Count de Volney, 8 February 1805, in *Jefferson Papers*, Library of Congress, Washington, D.C.

45   Louis Greenbaum, "Thomas Jefferson, the Paris Hospitals, and the University of Virginia," *Eighteenth-Century Studies* 26, no. 4 (1993): 609.

46   Colin Jones and Michael Sonenscher, "The Social Functions of the Hospital in Eighteenth-Century France: The Case of the Hotel-Dieu of Nimes," *French Historical Studies* 13, no. 2 (1983): 173.

47   Greenbaum, "Jefferson, Hospitals, University of Virginia," 610.

48   James Buchanan and William Hay to Thomas Jefferson, 20 March 1785, in *The Papers of Thomas Jefferson*, vol. 8, ed. Julian Boyd (Princeton: Princeton University Press, 1953), 49.

49   Hence the word penitentiary, a reform strongly advocated by the Quakers in Pennsylvania.

50   Harold Kalman, "Newgate Prison," *Architectural History* 12 (1969): 56.

51   *Ibid.*

52   Thomas Jefferson to James Buchanan and William Hay, 13 August 1785, in *The Papers of Thomas Jefferson*, vol. 8, ed. Julian Boyd (Princeton: Princeton University Press, 1953), 368.

53   Thomas Jefferson to David Humphreys, 14 August 1787, in *The Papers of Thomas Jefferson*, vol. 12, ed. Julian Boyd (Princeton: Princeton University Press, 1955), 32.

54   Greenbaum, "Jefferson, Hospitals, University of Virginia," 610.

55   *Ibid.*

56   Mary Woods, "Thomas Jefferson and the University of Virginia: Planning the Academic Village," *The Journal of the Society of Architectural Historians* 44, no. 3 (1985): 275.

57   *Ibid.*, 276.

58   Jefferson had a copy of du Pont's paper, "Ideas on the Nature, Form and Extent of Assistance to Give the Sick Poor in a Large City," in his library. E. M. Sowerby, Catalogue of the Library of Thomas Jefferson, vol. 3 (Washington, D.C.: U.S. Government Printing Office, 1952), 2386n; Greenbaum, "Jefferson, Hospitals, University of Virginia," 610n.

59   Jean-Sylvain Bailley, "Extrait des registres de l'Academie royale des sciences, du 22 Novembre 1786. Rapport des commissaries chargés par l'Academie de l'examen du projet d'un nouvel

Hotel-Dieu, 1786," in *The Papers of Thomas Jefferson*, vol. 11, ed. Julian Boyd (Princeton: Princeton University Press, 1955), 43n.

60   Thomas Jefferson to Louis Guillaume Otto, 14 January 1787, in *The Papers of Thomas Jefferson*, vol. 11, ed. Julian Boyd (Princeton: Princeton University Press, 1955), 42.

61   In W. B. O'Neal, *Jefferson's Buildings at the University of Virginia: The Rotunda* (Charlottesville: University of Virginia Press, 1960), 1.

62   Greenbaum, "Jefferson, Hospitals, University of Virginia," 611.

63   Thomas Jefferson to Joseph Priestley, 18 January 1800, in *The Papers of Thomas Jefferson*, vol. 31, ed. Barbara Oberg (Princeton: Princeton University Press, 2004), 320.

64   Thomas Jefferson to the Trustee for the Lottery of East Tennessee College, 6 May 1810, in *The Complete Jefferson*, ed. Saul Padover (New York: Tudor, 1943), 1063.

65   *Ibid.*

66   *Ibid.*; cf. "to be adjusted to any number of prisoners, small or great and admitting an execution from time to time as it may be convenient." Thomas Jefferson to James Buchanan and William Hay, 13 August 1785, in *The Papers of Thomas Jefferson*, vol. 8, ed. Julian Boyd (Princeton: Princeton University Press, 1953), 368.

67   Thomas Jefferson to Wilson Cary Nicholas, 2 April 1816, in *Jefferson Papers*, Library of Congress, Washington, D.C.

68   Greenbaum, "Jefferson, Hospitals, University of Virginia," 623.

69   Woods, "Planning the Academic Village," 282.

CHAPTER 5: *Jefferson the Scientific Spymaster*

1   "Fearing infringements from early in their association Small wrote Watt explicit directions for the patent phraseology in 1769. Industrial spies were everywhere, Boulton particularly feared the French. The Russians had no qualms about raiding British brain power and goods. Catherine the Great herself made a visit to the Birmingham Lunar Society and both Small and Watt had received offers to work in St. Petersburg. Boulton is thought to have maintained a large spy network that would improvise on industrial secrets borrowed especially from his French and German counterparts as well as from his own countrymen and even friends." Martin Clagett, "William Small, 1734–1775: Teacher, Mentor, Scientist" (PhD diss., Virginia Commonwealth University, 2003), 236; see also William Small to James Watt, 5 February 1769. JWP 4/24, Archives, Birmingham Public Library, Birmingham, England.

2   Francis Fauquier to the Board of Trade, 5 January 1759, in *The Official Papers of Francis Fauquier*, vol. 1, ed. George Reese (Charlottesville: University of Virginia Press, 1981), 384. "The Manner in which this Order and Instruction were deliver'd to me, appeared to me so unusual and extraordinary ... The copies of these papers have been sent in the Colony above these six Months, they were sent to Mr. Camm's Friends, and have been communicated to many ... a Step unprecedented, of pernicious Consequence, and a high Insult to his Majesty." See also Francis Fauquier to Samuel Nicolls, 29 July 1761, in *The Official Papers of Francis Fauquier*, vol. 2, ed. George Reese (Charlottesville: University of Virginia Press, 1981), 552.

3   Thomas Jefferson to John Page, 15 July 1763, in *The Papers of Thomas Jefferson*, vol. 1, ed. Julian Boyd (Princeton: Princeton University Press, 1950), 11.

4   Thomas Jefferson to John Page, 23 January 1764, in *The Papers of Thomas Jefferson*, vol. 1, ed. Julian Boyd (Princeton: Princeton University Press, 1950), 15.

5   Thomas Jefferson to William Fleming, October 1763, in *The Papers of Thomas Jefferson*, vol. 1, ed. Julian Boyd (Princeton: Princeton University Press, 1950), 12. "I salute all the girls below in your name, particularly S_ _ _ _ _ Y   P _ _ _ _ R."

6   Thomas Jefferson to John Walker, 3 September 1763, in *The Papers of Thomas Jefferson*, vol. 1, ed. Julian Boyd (Princeton: Princeton University Press, 1950), 32. "*successor dignus dignissimi parvi!*"– "A worthy successor of the most worthy Small," Parvus being the Latin for Jefferson's old professor, William Small.

7   Thomas Jefferson to John Page, 23 January 1764, in *The Papers of Thomas Jefferson*, vol. 1, ed. Julian Boyd (Princeton: Princeton University Press, 1950), 15.

8   Thomas Jefferson to John Walker, 3 September 1763, in *The Papers of Thomas Jefferson*, vol. 1, ed. Julian Boyd (Princeton: Princeton University Press, 1950), 32.

9   Thomas Jefferson to John Page, 23 January 1764, in *The Papers of Thomas Jefferson*, vol. 1, ed. Julian Boyd (Princeton: Princeton University Press, 1950), 15.

10   David Kahn, *The Codebreakers* (New York: Scribner, 1996), xvi.

11   Three types of invisible ink were in common usage during this period. The first was lead ink, which was made from a solution of lead combined with hydrogen sulphide; the second was a powder of bismuth mixed with ammonia water; and the third, and most common, was "gallo-tannic acid … obtained by soaking powdered nut-galls in water and developed by an iron sulphate soulution;" Sanborn Brown and Elbridge Stein, "Benjamin Thompson and the First Secret-Ink Letter of the American Revolution," *Journal of Criminal Law and Criminology* vol. 40, no. 5 (January – February 1950): 630.

12   Kahn, *Codebreakers*, 174.

13   In 1628, Henry II of France laid siege to the Huguenot town of Réalmont. An encrypted letter from the town was intercepted and a local scholar, Antoine Rossignol, immediately decoded it. The letter indicated that the rebels were running out of supplies and would have to capitulate if reinforcements did not arrive within the week. The next day, the besiegers presented the text of the message to the commander and the Huguenots surrendered. Réalmont fell and Cardinal Richelieu hired Rossignol as France's first full-time cryptographer. Rossignol's successes made him wealthy and famous. The King himself visited Rossignol several times at home and his position as the official decipherer was handed down to his son and grandson. Due to the increased volume of work provided by Richelieu and his successor Mazarin, Rossignol hired young talent and under the Minister of War, Louvais, he established an office in the central black chamber of the palace, which was referred to by the name Cabinet Noir.

14   Wallis had initially worked for the Parliamentary forces of Oliver Cromwell in deciphering messages sent between the Royalists and was compensated by them with offices and cash rewards. After the Restoration, "though Charles II knew of Wallis' parliamentary services … [he] found him so valuable that soon after he ascended the throne he was employing the man who recently worked against him." Kahn, *Codebreakers*, 167.

15   Ralph E. Weber, *United States Diplomatic Codes and Ciphers: 1775-1938* (Chicago: Precedent Publishing Co., 1979), 47.

16   A note encrypted with Greek letters was intercepted and passed on to General Washington, who, by interrogation of the messenger, determined the sender to be Dr. Benjamin Church, the Director General of Hospitals and a leader in the Massachusetts Congress. Church refused to decode the letter and Washington sent it separately to Reverend West and Eldridge Gerry. Both sources independently returned the same translation, which included among other sensitive information the proposed American plan of attack on Canada, American troop strength in Philadelphia, and the low state of American ammunition. Other turncoat cryptographers included Benedict Arnold, Edward Bancroft, and Benjamin Thompson. David Kiracofe, "Dr. Benjamin Church and the Dilemma of Treason in Revolutionary Massachusetts," *The New England Quarterly* 70, no. 3 (1997): 443–462; Michael Peterson, "The Church Cryptogram" in Ralph Weber, *Masked Dispatches: Cryptograms and Cryptology on American History*, 1775-1900 (Ft. Meade, MD: National Security Agency, 2002), 25–30.

17   Weber, *Codes and Ciphers*, 107.

18   William C. Bruce, *Benjamin Franklin: Self Revealed*, vol. 2 (New York: G. P. Putnam's Sons, 1917), 236; Ralph Weber, *Cryptograms and Cryptology*, 11.

19   Weber, *Codes and Ciphers*, 23.

20   *Ibid.*, 27.

21   *Ibid.*, 35.

22   *Ibid.*, 37.

23   *Ibid.*, 36.

24   *Ibid.*, 39.

25   *Ibid.*

26.   *Ibid.* A code not used by Jefferson but current during this time was perhaps inspired by Napoleon's Egyptian Campaign. William Vans Murray, who conducted negotiations with the French during the Adams administration, developed a cipher which included symbols, or hieroglyphics as some dubbed them. The system was so simplified that even so inept a cryptographer as John Adams could use it with some satisfaction.

27   Robert Patterson to Thomas Jefferson, 19 December 1801, in *Jefferson Papers*, Library of Congress, Washington, D.C.

28   Weber, *Cryptograms and Cryptology*, 74.

29   Thomas Jefferson to Robert Patterson, 22 March 1802, in *Jefferson Papers*, Library of Congress, Washington, D.C.

30 Weber, *Codes and Ciphers*, 151.

31 *Ibid.*, 102.

32 *Ibid.*, 151.

33 "Notes prepared by Julian Boyd," Item 35054, Harrison Institute, Albert and Shirley Small Collection, University of Virginia, Charlottesville, VA.

34 *Ibid.*

35 "Thomas Jefferson Cipher Codes used for Diplomatic Correspondence," Accession # 38-285, TB 56, Special Collections, Harrison Institute, Albert and Shirley Small Collection, University of Virginia, Charlottesville, VA.

36 John Adams, who was deeply engaged in numerous diplomatic negotiations both as a minister and as president, was continually confounded by the complexities of the codes. Abigail Adams wrote James Lovell in 1780 that she hated "a cipher of any kind" and "Besides my Friend (John Adams) is no adept in investigating ciphers and hates to be puzzeld for a meaning." Weber, *Codes and Ciphers*, 30; John Adams wrote to Lovell in frustration, "[I] have made my alphabet accordingly; but I am on this occasion, as on all others hitherto, unable to comprehend the sense of the passages in cypher … I have been able sometimes to decypher words enough to show that I have the letters right; but, upon the whole, I can make nothing of it, which I regret very much upon this occasion, as I suppose the cyphers are a very material part of the letter" (*Ibid.*, 31); John Adams's skills encoding messages were as poor as his skills decoding. In 1799, William Vans Murray informed Adams that he was unable to make out his new cipher. Adams apologized, "My poor cypher! I meant to make it complicated & increase the difficulty of deciphering. And Lo! I made it unintelligible to my own correspondent" (*Ibid.*, 142); The ineptitude of Adams in this regard was so well known that the minister to Russia, Francis Dana, designed a simplified code in order to accommodate him, and when this also proved troublesome, Dana suggested the dictionary code along with a brief code list (*Ibid.*, 65).

37 Weber, *Codes and Ciphers*, 157.

38 *Ibid.*, 32.

39 Benjamin Franklin to Robert Livingston, 5 December 1782, in *The Revolutionary Diplomatic Correspondence of the United States*, vol. 4 (Washington, D.C.: Government Printing Office, 1889), 110–111.

40 *Ibid.*

41 Weber, *Codes and Ciphers*, 73.

42 One of the first book codes used in the Revolutionary War was conducted between Benedict Arnold and John Andre, a young British major. The text used was *Blackstone's Commentaries* but the conspirators soon ran into problems as few of the encoded words could be found whole and "most of the words and proper names had to be spelled out in an enormously cumbersome fashion that required tedious counting for each letter … Arnold consequently abandoned the system after sending one message." Andre and Arnold next hit upon the idea of using a best-selling dictionary, the *Universal Etymological English Dictionary* by Nathan Bailey, because of the expanded number of options for whole words and because the alphabetic listing made those words easier to find. The dictionary seemed to be the pragmatic answer, and the most widely used spy codebook was John Entick's *New Spelling Dictionary*. Kahn, *Codebreakers*, 177.

43 Weber, *Codes and Ciphers*s, 52.

44 *Ibid.*, 48.

45 Kahn, *Codebreakers*, 181.

46 *Ibid.*, 177.

47 *Ibid.*, 183.

48 Weber, *Codes and Ciphers*, 56.

49 Weber, *Cryptograms and Cryptology*, 55; quoque 56n.

50 James Jay wrote to Jefferson, "When the affairs of America … began to wear a serious aspect, and threatened to issue in civil war, it occurred to me that a fluid might possibly be discovered for invisible writing, which would elude the generally known means of detection, and yet could be rendered visible by a suitable counterpart." James Jay continued that in order to avoid suspicion that would arise if he wrote only to his brother John, a member of Congress, he also wrote to several other members of the family residing in America; he said he wrote three or four lines in black ink and "the residue of the blank page I filled up, invisibly, with such intelligence and matters as I thought would be useful to the American Cause." In Kahn, *Codebreakers*, 179; Jay furnished General Washington with both a liquid solution of invisible ink and a preparation that rendered it visible. Washington called it "white ink" or stain and wrote in July 1779, "All

the white Ink I now have (indeed all that there is any prospect of getting soon) is sent in phial No. 1 by Col. Webb. The liquid in No. 2 is the counterpart which renders the other visible by wetting the paper with a fine brush after the first has been used and dried" (*Ibid.*); *vide quoque* Weber, *Codes and Ciphers*, 109n9; George Washington to Benjamin Tallmadge, 25 July 1779, in George Washington, *The Writings of George Washington from Original Manuscript Sources, 1745–1799*, vol. 15, ed. John Fitzpatrick (Washington, D.C.: Government Printing Office, 1938), 483; James Jay informed Jefferson that by this subterfuge he was able both to alert the American Congress that, despite feinted overtures of reconciliation, the British ministry had already determined to reduce the colonies to unconditional surrender and make known to Franklin the British plans to send an expedition from Canada under General Burgoyne. Kahn, *Codebreakers*, 179. Moreover, the Americans were not the only ones to use this medium, for within a few weeks of the Battle of Lexington, the notorious American traitor Benjamin Thompson sent a letter partially written in invisible ink to the British command in Boston. Sanborn Brown and Elbridge Stein, "Benjamin Thompson and the First Secret Ink Letter of the American Revolution," *Journal of Criminal Law and Criminology* 40, no. 5 (January–February 1950): 627. Thompson used a gallotannic acid invented by Jean Baptista Porta in 1480 and ferrous sulphate as its developer. The letter revealed the rebel plans to dislodge the British forces in Boston: "The first movement will be a feint attack upon the Town of Boston, & at the same time to attempt the Castle with the main body of the Army" (*Ibid.*, 628).

51 Weber, *Codes and Ciphers*, 118.

52 Silvio Bedini, *Jefferson and the Sciences* (Chapel Hill: University of North Carolina Press, 2002), 77.

53 Kahn, *Codebreakers*, 194.

54 Silvio Bedini, *Thomas Jefferson: Statesman of Science* (New York: Macmillan, 1990), 239.

55 Bedini, *Jefferson and the Sciences*, 78.

56 Girolamo Cardano, *De Subtilitate Libri XXI* (Basciliae: apud J. Petreium, 1560), 1074–1076, in Louis Kruh, "The Genesis of the Jefferson-Bazeries Cipher Device," *Cryptologia* 5, no. 4 (1981), 207n45.

57 *Encyclopédie Ancienne*, vol. 2 (Paris: M. Diderot, 1751), 512, in Louis Kruh, "The Genesis of the Jefferson-Bazeries Cipher Device," *Cryptologia* 5, no. 4 (1981), 207n72.

58 *Encyclopédie Ancienne: Recueil de Planches*, vol. 9 (Paris: M. Diderot, 1771), plate XXX in Louis Kruh, "The Genesis of the Jefferson-Bazeries Cipher Device," *Cryptologia* 5, no. 4 (1981), 208n73.

59 *Encyclopédie Méthodique, Tome Quatrième, Recueil de Planches de L'Encyclopédie* (Paris: Chez Panckoucke, 1785), 99, in Louis Kruh, "The Genesis of the Jefferson-Bazeries Cipher Device," *Cryptologia* 5, no. 4 (1981), 207n54.

60 *Encyclopédie Méthodique, Tome Septième, Arts et Métiers Mécaniques* (Paris: Chez Panckoucke, 1790), 471–473, in Louis Kruh, "The Genesis of the Jefferson-Bazeries Cipher Device," *Cryptologia* 5, no. 4 (1981), 207 n56.

61 *Catalogue of the Library of Thomas Jefferson*, vol. 5, ed. Millicent Sowerby (Washington, D.C.: Government Printing Office, 1959), 149.

62 Rudolf Kippenhahn, *Code Breaking: A History and Exploration* (New York: Overlook Press, 1999), 28–29.

63 Bedini, *Jefferson and the Sciences*, 80.

64 *Ibid.*, 82; In 1922, Dr. John M. Manly, a Chaucer scholar, cryptanalyst, and head of the Department of English at the University of Chicago, analyzed two pages of a holographic manuscript from the Jefferson Papers in the Library of Congress entitled "The Wheel Cipher." The description of the device matched very closely to both the Bazerier model developed in the 1890s and the American improvements of Captain Hitt and General Mauborgne's design in the second decade of the twentieth century. William F. Friedman, *The Friedman Legacy: Six Lectures on Cryptology* (Ft. Meade: National Security Agency, 1992), 192.

65 Bedini, *Jefferson and the Sciences*, 82.

66 Bedini, *Statesman*, 242.

67 Kahn, *Codebreakers*, 192.

68 *Ibid.*, 195.

69 Among those distinguished authorities are William Friedman, Louis Kruh, Silvio Bedini, David Kahn, Ralph Weber, *inter alios*.

70 Jack Ingram in discussion with Martin Clagett, 12 September 2007; Mr. Earl Coates in discussion with Martin Clagett, 20 September 2007; Mr. George Lower in discussion with Martin Clagett, 21 September 2007; Chad Wollerton in discussion with Martin Clagett, 21 September 2007.

71   David Gaddy, "The Cylinder-Cipher," *Cryptologia* 19, no. 4 (October 1995): 387–388.

72   Jack Ingram (former curator of the National Cryptologic Museum) in discussion with Martin Clagett, 12 Sepember 2007.

73   Louis Kruh, "The Genesis of the Jefferson-Bazeries Cipher Device," *Cryptologia* 5, no. 4 (October 1981): 197.

CONCLUSION

1   John Page, "Memoir of Governor Page," *Virginia Historical Register and Literary Note Book*, vol. 3, no. 1 (1850), 150. Page's obsession was so profound that Jefferson, in a rare moment of humor, wrote, "Why the devil don't you write? But I suppose that you are on the moon, or some of the planetary regions … If your spirit is too elevated to advert to sublunary subjects, depute my friend Mrs. Page to support your correspondencies." Thomas Jefferson to John Page, 21 February 1770, in *The Papers of Thomas Jefferson*, vol. 1, ed. Julian Boyd (Princeton: Princeton University Press, 1950), 35.

2   Thomas Jefferson to Thomas Jefferson Randolph, 24 November 1808, in *The Writings of Thomas Jefferson*, vol. 9, ed. Paul L. Ford (New York: G. P. Putnam's Sons, 1898), 231.

3   Devereux Jarratt, *The Life of the Reverend Devereux Jarratt* (Baltimore: Warner and Hanna, 1806), 17; R. A. Brock values the pistol at $3.60. R. A. Brock, *The Official Records of Robert Dinwiddie* (Richmond: Virginia Historical Society, 1883), 44. Noted colonial historian Jack Green estimates $4.00. Jack Greene, "Landon Carter and the Pistole Fee Dispute," *William and Mary Quarterly* 14, no. 1 (1957): 210. A contemporary source gives the value as 16 Shillings, 6 pence. James Abercromby, *The Letter Books of James Abercromby, Colonial Agent, 1751–1773*, eds. John Van Horne and George Reese (Richmond: Virginia State Library, 1991), 60n.

4   Silvio Bedini. *Thomas Jefferson: Statesman of Science* (New York: Macmillan, 1990), 206.

5   Thomas Jefferson, March 1784, in *The Papers of Thomas Jefferson*, vol. 7, ed. Julian Boyd (Princeton: Princeton University Press, 1953), 175–185.

6   Bedini, *Statesman*, 205.

7   *Ibid.*

8   *Ibid.*, 210.

9   George Hastings, "Notes on the Beginnings of Aeronautics in America," *The American Historical Review* 25, no. 1 (October 1919): 68.

10   Bedini, *Statesman*, 231.

11   Thomas Jefferson to Martha Jefferson Randolph, 14 January 1793, in *The Papers of Thomas Jefferson*, vol. 25, ed. John Catanzariti (Princeton: Princeton University Press, 1992), 50.

12   Thomas Jefferson to Francis Hopkinson, 18 February 1784, in *The Papers of Thomas Jefferson*, vol. 6, ed. Julian Boyd (Princeton: Princeton University Press, 1952), 542. Hopkinson responded, "We have not taken the affair of Balloons in hand. A high flying Politician is, I think, not unlike a Balloon—he is full of inflammability, he is driven along by every current of the wind and those who suffer themselves to be carried along by them run a great Risk that the Bubble may burst and let them fall from the Height to which the Principle of Levity has raised them." Francis Hopkinson to Thomas Jefferson, 12 March 1784, in *The Papers of Thomas Jefferson* vol. 7, ed. Julian Boyd (Princeton: Princeton University Press, 1953), 20.

13   Thomas Jefferson to Francis Hopkinson, 18 February 1784, in *The Papers of Thomas Jefferson*, vol. 6, ed. Julian Boyd (Princeton: Princeton University Press, 1952), 542.

14   Thomas Jefferson to Robert Fulton, 21 July 1813, in *Writings of Thomas Jefferson*, vol. 5, ed. H. A. Washington (Washington, D.C.: Taylor & Maury, 1853), 165.

15   D. Bushnell, "General Principles and Construction of a Sub-marine Vessel, communicated by D. Bushnell of Connecticut, the inventor, in a letter of October, 1787, to Thomas Jefferson then Minister Plenipotentiary of the United States at Paris," *Transactions of the American Philosophical Society*, vol. 4, no. 37 (1799), 303, from Special Collections, Harrison Institute, University of Virginia, Charlottesville, Va.

16   *Ibid.*, 304.

17   *Ibid.*, 307–308.

18   *Ibid.*, 312.

19   Thomas Jefferson to Robert Fulton, 16 August 1807, in *The Writings of Thomas Jefferson*, vol. 9, ed. Paul L. Ford (New York: G. P. Putnam's Sons, 1898), 125.

20 *Ibid.*

21 Alex Roland, "Science and War," *Osiris*, 2nd ser., 1 (1985): 252.

22 Julia Macleod, "Jefferson and the Navy: A Defense," *The Huntington Library Quarterly* 8, no. 2 (February 1945): 180.

23 Thomas Jefferson to Lewis Wiss, 27 November 1825, in *Writings of Thomas Jefferson*, vol. 7, ed. H. A. Washington (Washington, D.C.: Taylor & Maury, 1854), 419.

24 *Ibid.*

25 *Ibid.*

26 Macleod, "Jefferson and the Navy," 170. See also *Writings of Thomas Jefferson*, vol. 7, ed. H. A. Washington (Washington, D.C.: Taylor & Maury, 1854), 421.

27 Thomas Jefferson to Lewis Wiss, 27 November 1825. *Writings of Thomas Jefferson*, vol. 7, ed. H. A. Washington (Washington, D.C.: Taylor & Maury, 1854), 421.

28 Elizabeth Chew (Assistant Curator, Monticello) in correspondence with Martin Clagett, 4 August 2007.

29 Silvio Bedini, "Thomas Jefferson: Clock Designer," *Proceedings of the American Philosophical Society* 108, no. 3 (1964): 166; *Jefferson Papers* 233, folio 41588, "The Great Clock" Manuscript Division, Library of Congress, Washington, D.C.

30 Bedini, *Statesman*, 328.

31 Insert from Jacob Rubsamen, 1 December 1780, in *The Papers of Thomas Jefferson*, vol. 4, ed. Julian Boyd (Princeton: Princeton University Press, 1951), 174. Rubsamen added, "He was much pleased with a fancy Painting of mine and particularly admired the Paper Money brought on in the piece, and in Joke often rebuked me for my thoughtlessness to shew him counterfeit money for wich I Knew many had been hanged allready."

32 Watt used his copying machine to record both personal and business correspondence. One of the largest collections of documents is the Boulton-Watt Collection in the Birmingham Public Library. The combined collection, due to Watt's copy machine, is so large that the actual number of documents is estimated to be between two and four million pieces. Tim Procter (Project Manager for the Boulton-Watt Collection) in correspondence with Martin Clagett, 5 November 2002.

33 Bedini, *Statesman*, 117. Franklin evidently bought Watt's machine in the early 1780s and told Jefferson about it. Jefferson then ordered a machine: "Among the Franklin Papers is a letter from the London firm of Herries & Co. to William Temple Franklin, 13 April 1784, acknowledging an order forwarded by Franklin on 3 April 1784 from Robert Morris for a 'Copying Machine with paper &c for Mr. Jefferson' to be sent 'by the first opportunity to Virginia.'" *The Papers of Thomas Jefferson*, vol. 6, ed. Julian Boyd (Princeton: Princeton University Press, 1952), 373.

34 *Jefferson's Memorandum Books*, vol. 1, eds. James Bear and Lucia Stanton (Princeton: Princeton University Press, 1997), 622; "Pd. Woodmason for damping box, paper, &c. 10/." James Woodmason, Stationer at No. 5 Leadenhall Street, was agent for the Watt copying presses and their apparatus.

35 One of the stops in Birmingham included a visit to an office for "mechanical picture." (*Ibid.*, 619) This office may have been located at Boulton's Soho Factory, where Jefferson would likely have viewed Watt's Copy Presses. Boulton produced in one branch of his firm devices "to produce mechanical pictures" from which Watt may have developed his copy presses. Silvio Bedini, *Thomas Jefferson and His Copying Machines* (Charlottesville: University of Virginia Press, 1984), 11.

36 Bedini, *Statesman*, 331.

37 Thomas Jefferson to Charles Thomson, 17 December 1786, in *The Papers of Thomas Jefferson*, vol. 10, ed. Julian Boyd (Princeton: Princeton University Press, 1954), 608–610; Thomas Jefferson to Charles Thomson, 22 April 1786, in *The Papers of Thomas Jefferson*, vol. 9, ed. Julian Boyd (Princeton: Princeton University Press, 1953), 400–401.

38 Thomas Jefferson to Charles Thomson, 22 April 1786, in *The Papers of Thomas Jefferson*, vol. 9, ed. Julian Boyd (Princeton: Princeton University Press, 1954), 400.

39 *Ibid.*, 401n; Fiona Tait (Archivist, Birmingham Public Library) in communication with Martin Clagett, 17 August 2007.

40 Thomas Jefferson to Charles Thomson, 17 December 1786, in *The Papers of Thomas Jefferson*, vol. 10, ed. Julian Boyd (Princeton: Princeton University Press, 1954), 609.

41 Bedini, *Statesman*, 263.

42   Thomas Jefferson, undated entry in his building notebook, in Susan Stein and John Rudder, "Lighting Jefferson's Monticello," *PTB Bulletin* 31, no. 1 (2000): 21.

43   "The three-sash windows he had built at floor level were also designed to be converted into doorways by raising the two bottom sashes to the top one. To many of the window casings he added hidden shutters." Bedini, *Statesman*, 406.

44   Stein and Rudder, "Lighting Monticello," 22.

45   *Ibid.*, 21; Elizabeth Chew in personal communication with Martin Clagett, 16 August 2007.

46   Benjamin Thomson, who was the first known American to use invisible ink in transmitting secret messages during the Revolutionary War, was rewarded by both the British and the Elector of Bavaria. He married the widow of the French chemist Lavoisier, became a member of the Royal Society, and established an endowment for the American Philosophical Society. *vide quoque* Sanborn Brown and Elbridge Stein, "Benjamin Thompson and the First Secret-Ink Letter of the American Revolution," *Journal of Criminal Law and Criminology* 40, no. 5 (January February 1950): 627–636; Sanborn Brown and Kenneth Scott, "Count Rumford: International Informer," *The New England Quarterly* 21, no. 1 (March 1948): 34–49; Allen French, *General Gage's Informers* (Ann Arbor: University of Michigan Press, 1932).

47   Edmund Randolph, "Edmond Randolph's Essay on the Revolutionary History of Virginia," *The Virginia Magazine of History and Biography* XLIII (1935): 122.

48   Silvio Bedini, *Thomas Jefferson and American Vertebrate Paleontology* (Charlottesville: Commonwealth of Virginia, 1985), 1; Gilbert Chinard, *Thomas Jefferson: Apostle of Americanism* (Boston: Little, Brown, 1929), 118; Bedini, *Statesman*, 494.

49   Jeffrey Hantman and Gary Dunham, "The Enlightened Archaeologist," *Archaeology* 46 (May–June 1993), 46; See also David Bushnell, "The Indian Grave–A Monacan Site in Albemarle County, Virginia," *William and Mary Quarterly* 23, no. 2 (October 1914): 106–112. The author sent Jefferson's description of the gravesite verbatim, without revealing the author, to Derek Alexander, Senior Archaeologist for the National Trust, Western Scotland, for evaluation. Alexander replied, "This reads like quite an old fashioned report! I take it is. Sounds like they know more about bones than archaeological techniques. When was it written? Not in a position to judge competence–but if there are associated plans and section drawings and photographs then this might be more helpful." Derek Alexander in personal communication with Martin Clagett, 25 June 2007.

50   "Both by reason of his published opinions and by his actual investigations, Thomas Jefferson is entitled to rank among the forerunners of the American School of Anthropologists." Alexander Chamberlain, "Thomas Jefferson's Ethnological Opinions and Activities," *American Anthropologist* 9, no. 3 (July 1907), 509.

51   Sidney Forman, "Why the United States Military Academy was Established in 1802," *Military Affairs* 29, no. 1 (Spring 1965), 28.

52   G. T. Rude, "The Survey of the Continental Shelf," *The Scientific Monthly* 34, no. 6 (June 1932), 547.

53   Herman Friis, "A Brief Review of the Development and Status of the Geographical and Cartographical Activities of the United States Government: 1776–1818," *Imago Mundi* 19 (1965), 70.

54   August Miller, "Jefferson as an Agriculturist," *Agricultural History* 16, no. 2 (April 1942), 77.

55   Bedini, *Statesman*, 449.

56   Thomas Jefferson to George Rogers Clark, 4 December 1783, in *The Papers of Thomas Jefferson*, vol. 6, ed. Julian Boyd (Princeton: Princeton University Press, 1952), 371.

57   Thomas Jefferson to John Paul Jones, 5 September 1785, in *The Papers of Thomas Jefferson*, vol. 8, ed. Julian Boyd (Princeton: Princeton University Press, 1953), 492.

58   Thomas Jefferson, "Autobiography," in *The Complete Jefferson,* ed. Saul Padover (New York: Tudor Publishing Co., 1943), 1163.

59   Thomas Jefferson to Charles Thomson, 20 September 1787, in *The Papers of Thomas Jefferson*, vol. 12, ed. Julian Boyd (Princeton: Princeton University Press, 1955), 159.

60   Thomas Jefferson, "Biographical Sketches. Meriweather Lewis," April 1813, in *The Complete Jefferson*, ed. Saul Padover (New York: Publishing Co., 1943), 909.

61   Thomas Jefferson, *"Autobiography,"* in *Thomas Jefferson: Writings*, ed. Merrill Peterson (New York: Library of America, 1984), 61–62. If that path was not available, Ledyard proposed "to go to Kentucke, and thence penetrate Westwardly to the South Sea." Thomas Jefferson to Ezra Stiles, 1 September 1786 in *The Papers of Thomas Jefferson*, vol. 10, ed. Julian Boyd (Princeton: Princeton University Press, 1954), 316.

62 Thomas Jefferson to the Rev. James Madison, 19 July 1788, in *The Papers of Thomas Jefferson*, vol. 13, ed. Julian Boyd (Princeton: Princeton University Press, 1956), 382.

63 Thomas Jefferson to André Michaux, 23 January 1793, "Instructions for Exploring the Western Boundary," in *The Complete Jefferson*, ed. Saul Padover (New York: Tudor, 1943), 257.

64 *Ibid.*

65 Thomas Jefferson to Meriwether Lewis, 20 June 1803, "Expedition to the Pacific: Instructions to Captain Lewis," in *Thomas Jefferson: Writings*, ed. Merrill Peterson (New York: Library of America, 1984), 1127.

66 *Ibid.*

67 *Ibid.*, 1128.

68 Thomas Jefferson to Thomas Cooper, 25 August 1814, in *Writings of Thomas Jefferson*, vol. 6, ed. H. A. Washington (Washington, D.C.: Taylor & Maury, 1854), 371.

69 Thomas Jefferson, Bill No. 80, *The Papers of Thomas Jefferson*, vol. 2, ed. Julian Boyd (Princeton: Princeton University Press, 1950), 540.

70 All the plans for revision seem to have met with apathy and neglect. The President of William and Mary wrote despairingly, "The Visitors seem to have abandoned the College. We have not been able to obtain a Meeting of them for 5 Years. Such is the attention paid to Science!" Bishop James Madison to Thomas Jefferson, 17 January 1800, in *The Papers of Thomas Jefferson*, vol. 31, ed. Barbara Oberg (Princeton: Princeton University Press, 2004), 316.

71 Thomas Jefferson to Joseph Priestley, 18 January 1800, in *The Papers of Thomas Jefferson*, vol. 31, ed. Barbara Oberg (Princeton: Princeton University Press, 2004), 320.

72 "Extrait des registres de l'Académie royale des Sciences du 22 novembre, 1786" (109–115), in Louis Greenbaum, "Thomas Jefferson, the Paris Hospitals, and the University of Virginia," *Eighteenth Century Studies* vol. 26, no. 4 (Summer 1993), 611.

73 Louis Greenbaum, "Thomas Jefferson, the Paris Hospitals, and the University of Virginia," *Eighteenth Century Studies* vol. 26, no. 4 (Summer 1993), 618.

74 Thomas Jefferson to Joseph Priestley, 18 January 1800, in *The Papers of Thomas Jefferson*, vol. 31, ed. Barbara Oberg (Princeton: Princeton University Press, 2004), 320.

75 *Ibid.*, 321.

76 *Ibid.*

77 Joseph Priestley to Thomas Jefferson, 8 May 1800, in *The Papers of Thomas Jefferson*, vol. 31, ed. Barbara Oberg (Princeton: Princeton University Press, 2004), 568.

78 *Ibid.*

79 *Ibid.*

80 *Ibid.*, 569.

81 Thomas Jeffferson to John Harvie, 14 January 1760, in *The Papers of Thomas Jefferson*, vol. 1, ed. Julian Boyd (Princeton: Princeton University Press, 1950), 3.

82 "May.22: 2 hands grubbed the Grave yard 80.f.sq = 1/7 of an acre in 3 ? hours so that one would have done it in 7. Hours, and would grub an acre in 49.hours = 4. Days." in *Thomas Jefferson's Garden Book: 1766–1824*, ed. E. Morris Betts (Charlottesville: Thomas Jefferson Memorial Foundation, 1999), 40.

83 Thomas Jefferson to Duc de Marbois, 5 December 1783, in *The Papers of Thomas Jefferson*, vol. 6, ed. Julian Boyd (Princeton: Princeton University Press, 1952), 374.

Index

References are to pages. Preface pages are in roman type. Italicized pages indicate figures.